GOOD EATING

BAKING

GOOD EATING

BAKING

YOUR COMPLETE GUIDE TO PERFECT CAKES AND BAKED GOODS EVERY TIME

This edition published in 2011

LOVE FOOD is an imprint of Parragon Books Ltd

Parragon
Queen Street House
4 Queen Street
Bath BA1 1HE, UK

ISBN 978-1-4454-3955-6

Printed in China

Cover design by Talking Design
Internal design by Simon Levy
Photography by Clive Streeter
Food styling by Angela Drake and Teresa Goldfinch
Introduction and additional recipes by Christine France

This book uses imperial, metric, and US cup measurements. Follow the same units of
measurement throughout; do not mix imperial and metric. All spoon measurements are
level: teaspoons are assumed to be 5 ml, and tablespoons are assumed to be 15 ml. Unless
otherwise stated, milk is assumed to be whole, eggs and individual vegetables, such as
potatoes, are medium, and pepper is freshly ground black pepper.

The times given are an approximate guide only. Preparation times differ according to the
techniques used by different people and the cooking times may also vary from those
given as a result of the type of oven used. Optional ingredients, variations, or serving
suggestions have not been included in the calculations.

Recipes using raw or very lightly cooked eggs should be avoided by infants, the elderly,
pregnant women, convalescents, and anyone with a chronic condition. Pregnant and
breast-feeding women are advised to avoid eating peanuts and peanut products. People
with nut allergies should be aware that some of the prepared ingredients used in the
recipes in this book may contain nuts. Always check the package before use.

CONTENTS

GREASING & LINING PANS

For many simple sponge cakes you just need to give the bottom and sides of the pan a quick brush of oil or melted butter and insert a piece of nonstick parchment paper in the bottom. Richer or low-fat batters usually need a thoroughly greased and lined pan to prevent sticking.

Lining a round pan

1 Grease the pan. Cut a strip of parchment paper about 1 inch/2.5 cm longer than the circumference and about 1 inch/2.5 cm deeper than the pan.

2 Fold up one long edge about $^1/_2$ inch/1 cm, then unfold leaving a crease.

3 Use scissors to snip cuts along the folded edge of the paper so that it can be eased into the pan to fit around the curve at the bottom.

4 Place the pan on a sheet of parchment paper and draw around it with a pencil to mark the size. Cut with scissors just inside the line, making a round to fit inside the bottom, covering the snipped edges of the side lining paper. Grease the paper.

Lining a square pan

1 Grease the pan. Cut a strip of parchment paper about 1 inch/2.5 cm longer than the circumference of the pan and 1 inch/2.5 cm deeper.

2 Fold up one long edge about $^1/_2$ inch/1 cm, then unfold leaving a crease. Fit the paper into the sides of the pan, cutting a diagonal slit into the folded edge to fit each corner.

3 Place the pan on a sheet of parchment paper, draw around it to mark the size, then cut just inside the line to make a square. Lay the square inside the pan, covering the folded edges. Grease the paper.

Lining a jelly roll pan or rectangular pan

1 Grease the bottom and sides of the pan. Cut a piece of parchment paper $2^3/_4$ inches/7 cm larger than the pan.

2 Place the pan on the paper, then make a cut from each corner of the paper in toward the pan corner.

3 Place the paper inside the pan so that the diagonally cut corners overlap and fit neatly. Grease the paper.

Lining a loaf pan

1 Grease the pan. Cut a strip of parchment paper the length of the pan bottom and wide enough to cover the bottom and long sides. Place the paper in the pan.

2 Cut a second piece of parchment paper the width of the pan bottom and long enough to cover the bottom and ends of the pan. Slot this in over the first piece to line the pan, then grease the paper.

Flouring pans

1 Grease the bottom and sides of the ban, then slip a piece of parchment paper in the bottom. Grease the paper.

2 Sprinkle a little flour into the pan. Tilt the pan, tapping lightly so the flour coats the bottom and sides evenly. Tip out any excess.

ADDITIONAL EQUIPMENT

Oven

A reliable oven is essential to successful baking, and it's a good idea to check yours regularly with an oven thermometer to make sure it's accurate. Preheat the oven to the required temperature for 10–15 minutes before use, so that it has time to fully reach the correct temperature. Fan ovens cook more quickly than conventional ovens, so cooking times can be reduced by 5–10 minutes per hour, or the temperature may be reduced slightly.

Avoid the temptation to keep opening the oven door to check on your cake, particularly early in the cooking time, because a sudden rush of cold air may cause the cake to sink.

Measuring cups

Metal and ceramic measuring cups are useful for measuring dry ingredients but less easy to use for liquids. Transparent glass or plastic cups are a good choice for measuring liquids, but make sure that they are heatproof. Choose ones with a good pouring lip and clear markings. Place the cup on a flat surface at eye level for accurate measuring of liquid ingredients.

Dry measuring cups are available in nested sets and usually include 2-cup, 1-cup, $^1/_2$-cup, $^1/_3$-cup, and $^1/_4$-cup sizes, and sometimes a $^1/_8$-cup (2-tablespoon) size. Although butter and brown sugar should be packed tightly into a measuring cup, all other ingredients should be placed into a measuring cup loosely. Unless otherwise stated, the ingredients in the cups should be level—you can use the straight back edge of a knife or your fingers to level off the ingredients.

Measuring spoons

It's important to use standard measuring spoons, measured level unless stated otherwise, because ordinary kitchen tablespoons and teaspoons can vary in size. In all the recipes in this book, a teaspoon is assumed to hold 5 ml and a tablespoon is assumed to hold 15 ml.

Electric mixer/food processor

A handheld electric mixer with a powerful motor can be used for creaming, whisking, blending, and kneading. Tabletop mixers, with greater capacity and more power, are useful for all mixtures, particularly large quantities.

Food processors can cream, blend, or knead, as well as doing other cooking tasks. Again, choose one with a powerful motor for durability. Be careful when using a food processor or powerful electric mixer for making cakes because they mix the ingredients very quickly. It is important not to overbeat cake mixtures because this will make their texture too dense.

Food processors are unsuitable for mixing meringues because the enclosed bowl does not hold enough air to give them volume.

Spoons

Wooden spoons are useful for creaming and mixing. Make sure you keep separate those used for cooking strongly flavored foods, such as onions, because wood can absorb flavors and may transfer them to more delicate mixtures. Heat-resistant nylon spoons are durable and less prone to absorbing flavors. A large metal spoon is useful for folding in ingredients.

Spatula

You'll find a flexible rubber or silicone spatula helpful for light mixing and scraping out bowls cleanly. Some have a spoon-shaped blade, which helps when transferring cake batter from the bowl to the pan.

Bowls

Different-size mixing bowls are essential, and a set of toughened glass bowls is a good basic start because they are durable, heatproof, and easy to clean. Melamine resin, plastic, and ceramic bowls often have pouring lips, and some have nonslip bottoms to grip the counter.

Wire cooling racks

A wire rack lets your cakes cool evenly and prevents condensation, which can cause soggy texture and poor keeping quality. They vary from a simple metal rectangle to expanding three-tier ones, which are useful for large batches of baking. Some have a nonstick coating for easier cleaning.

Sifter

A good-quality rustproof metal or nylon sifter is necessary for sifting together dry ingredients evenly, and a set of three sizes is useful. Even nylon ones are hard wearing and will stand boiling water, but metal ones are the most durable and will last for years.

Graters

A hard-wearing stainless steel box grater or flat "Microplane" type grater with a firm grip handle is good for grating citrus rind, cheese, apple, chocolate, nutmeg, etc. You'll need a fine, medium, and coarse grater. Some also have a slicing option.

Citrus squeezer/reamer

A sturdy plastic, metal, toughened glass, or ceramic squeezer is used for extracting juice from citrus fruits. For smooth juice you'll need one with a filter part to extract all the fibers from the juice. A wooden reamer squeezes out the juice by simply pushing into the halved fruit, but you may also get some seeds.

Rolling pin

For rolling pie and cookie doughs, a wooden rolling pin is a good tool and you can shape and cool tuiles on it, too. Marble, granite, or glass are more expensive but their cool smooth surface is good for rolling sticky mixtures.

Pastry brush

A pastry brush is the easiest way to grease cake pans evenly, and can also be used for applying glazes. They are available with natural bristles or more durable synthetic bristles.

Cookie cutters

A set of round cookie cutters, with either plain or fluted edges, is a good basic choice, preferably in metal. Later you can add fancy-shaped cutters. Make sure the cutting edge is sharp and the top edge is rolled to safeguard your fingers and keep the cutter rigid.

Pastry bag and tips

For decorative piping of frostings or soft mixtures, you'll need pastry bags and tips. Strong nylon or fabric bags are washable and reusable, or you can buy strong disposable bags to save work. A small selection of stainless steel tips should include a plain writing, small and large star, and plain large vegetable tips.

GLOSSARY OF BAKING TERMS

Baking blind

Baking a pie shell without filling. Place a round of parchment paper or wax paper in the pie shell and fill with dried beans, rice, or ceramic pie weights, then bake as the recipe instructs.

Beating

A method of vigorously agitating with a spoon, fork, or whisk, to combine ingredients evenly, to soften ingredients, such as butter, or to incorporate air into mixtures.

Creaming

To beat together mixtures of fat and sugar to soften to a pale, fluffy consistency, incorporating air into the mix to make a light, spongy cake, such as a layer cake.

Dredging

To sprinkle a mixture or surface generously with a dry ingredient, such as flour or confectioners' sugar, either using a sifter or a "dredger" pot, which has a top with holes for even sprinkling.

Dusting

To sprinkle a surface lightly with a dry ingredient, such as flour, confectioners' sugar, or spices, to give a thin coating, using a fine sifter or dredger to distribute evenly.

Folding in

A method of combining a creamed mixture with dry ingredients, or to incorporate whisked egg whites, so that as little air as possible is knocked out. Ideally, use a large metal spoon to cut and fold the dry ingredients through the mixture, agitating as little as possible to retain air bubbles for lightness.

Glazing

To brush a coating over a mixture, either before or after baking, to give a glossy appearance or improve the flavor. For instance, beaten egg or milk are used to glaze pastries and breads, and syrups or jams may be brushed over a cake top for an attractive finish.

Kneading

A process of pressing and stretching a dough, with the hands or a dough hook, to strengthen the gluten (the protein in wheat flour). This makes the gluten more elastic, enabling the dough to rise easily and giving an even texture to the finished product.

Piping

Forcing a soft cake or cookie mixture, or a frosting, from a pastry bag through a tip, usually to create a decorative shape or effect, such as stars, rosettes, or lines. Use a firm, even pressure for best results.

Punching down

This is a second kneading, usually done after the dough has been left to rise and before shaping, with the purpose of punching out any large air bubbles from the dough to guarantee an even-textured result.

Rising

To let a bread dough stand after shaping, usually in a warm place. This is done to allow the dough to rise and give the finished bread a good rise and a light, even texture.

Rubbing in

A method of incorporating fat, such as butter, into dry ingredients, such as flour, using the fingertips to rub the two together evenly. The fingertips are the coolest part of the hand, and a cool, light touch helps to give a short texture to pie dough, cookies, and cakes.

Sifting

To shake dry ingredients, such as flour, through a sifter to eliminate lumps and create a smooth texture. It can also help to evenly distribute any added rising agents or spices.

Whipping

A term used to describe the gentle beating of a mixture, usually with a mixer, to make it smooth or incorporate air. For example, it is used to thicken heavy cream, or make it stiff enough for piping.

Whisking

Rapidly beating a mixture using a hand whisk or electric whisk to incorporate and trap large amounts of air. This method is used for whisked sponge cakes, which rely totally on air for a light, open texture, and meringues, where egg whites are whisked until they are stiff enough to hold peaks.

TOP TIPS FOR PERFECT RESULTS

CAKES

The right ingredients

Avoid using lowfat spreads in cakes unless the recipe has been written specially for these, because they have a high moisture content and tend to create a heavy, poor-textured result with traditional recipes. Ordinary "tub" margarine and softened butter have 80 percent fat content, and these are best for all-in-one creamed mixtures.

Run out of self-rising flour? Make your own by adding $2^{1}/_{2}$ teaspoons of baking powder to every 2 cups all-purpose flour. Sift together thoroughly before use to make sure the rising agent is evenly distributed.

Easy mixing

Let butter or margarine come to room temperature and soften for at least 30 minutes before use to make it easy to cream.

Always use eggs at room temperature for baking, particularly in whisked mixtures. They will whisk to a larger volume when used at room temperature.

Preventing curdling

When adding eggs to a creamed mixture, always add them gradually at first and beat hard after each addition to prevent it from curdling. If cake batter does start to curdle, quickly beat in a tablespoon or two of flour, which should correct it.

How to tell when a cake is cooked

To check a **sponge cake**, press it lightly on top with your fingertips—it should feel springy to the touch and spring back without leaving an impression. Most cakes, particularly whisked sponges, will begin to shrink away from the side of the pan when they are cooked, so this is a good indication.

To test a **rich fruitcake**, remove from the oven and place on the counter, then listen closely to the cake. If you can hear the cake mixture sizzling, it needs more cooking. If you can't hear anything, it should be cooked.

The toothpick test is also a useful check—insert a toothpick into the center of the cake, then withdraw it quickly; if there is a residue of sticky mixture on the toothpick, then the cake needs more cooking. If it comes out clean, the cake is cooked.

Successful storage

Make sure that your cakes and baked goods are completely cooled before storing because any residual warmth may cause condensation that will result in mold developing on the cake.

Rich fruitcakes should store for months and will improve with keeping. Wrap closely in a double layer of wax paper, then overwrap with foil or a plastic bag. Store in a cool, dry place with an even temperature.

DOUGHS

Flaky pie dough

Make sure all your ingredients and utensils are really cold, because this helps to make a really light, crisp pastry.

Once the liquid has been added, handle the dough as lightly and as little as possible, or it will be difficult to handle and will become heavy when baked.

If possible, chill the dough after shaping to prevent shrinkage during cooking.

Puff pastry

Before baking, dampen the baking sheet with a water spray or rinse under the faucet; the water will turn to steam, which will help the pastry rise.

When glazing puff pastry, be careful to avoid brushing over the cut edges because this can ruin the rise.

Choux pastry

It's important to beat the mixture thoroughly after adding the eggs to incorporate as much air as possible for a really light pastry. You can use a handheld electric mixer for this.

Choux pastry freezes well raw, so choux pastry balls can be piped onto a baking sheet and frozen. Thaw completely before baking as in the recipe.

Filo dough

To prevent sheets of filo dough from drying out while you work, cover them with a sheet of plastic wrap, then with a lightly dampened dish towel. Do not let the damp dish towel come in contact with the dough because this will cause it to stick.

If possible, fillings for filo dough should be cooled before use, because warm mixtures may cause the dough to soften and make it difficult to shape.

How to line a tart pan or pie plate

1 Place the tart pan or pie plate on a baking sheet. Roll out the dough to a circle about 2 inches/5 cm larger than the pan.

2 Carefully roll the dough over the rolling pin and lift over the pan, then unroll it evenly without stretching.

3 Carefully ease the dough into the sides of the pan, using your fingertips to press right into the edges to fit the shape closely without an air gap.

4 Roll a rolling pin over the top of the pan to trim off the surplus dough. Alternatively, if using a plain-edged tart pan or pie plate, trim with a knife, then pinch the edges with your fingers for a fluted edge.

Baking blind

This is a method of partially baking dough for tarts before adding the filling to guarantee a crisp, evenly-cooked pie dough that doesn't rise up underneath.

1 Roll out the dough, use to line the tart pan, and trim the top edge by rolling a rolling pin over the top. Prick the bottom all over with a fork.

2 Cut a piece of parchment paper or wax paper about 2 3/4 inches/7 cm larger than the pan and place it inside the pie shell.

3 Half-fill the paper with dried beans or ceramic pie weights to weigh the dough down as it cooks.

4 Bake the pie shell as in the recipe, usually for about 10 minutes, then remove the paper and beans, and bake for an additional 5 minutes to dry out before adding the filling.

COOKIES

When making cookies from a soft mixture that will spread, allow at least 2³/₄ inches/7 cm between each one when placing the mix on the baking sheet to prevent the cookies from joining together as they bake.

To stamp out cookies cleanly with a cookie cutter, rub the edges of the cutter into flour before each cut to prevent the dough from sticking to the cutter.

When making cookies from a rolled-out dough, it's worth making double the quantity and freezing half—roll it into a sausage shape, overwrap with foil, and freeze for up to 3 months. To use, thaw for about an hour at room temperature, then slice and bake as usual.

To add extra fiber and texture to plain cookies, roll out on a counter dusted with oatmeal or bran instead of flour.

BREAD

Tips on baking with yeast

To make sure the water is at the correct temperature for the yeast, mix one-third boiling water with two-thirds cold water. It should feel tepid—neither cold nor hot to the touch.

When using active dry yeast, make sure you add it to the dry ingredients first; never mix with liquid as with conventional yeast. Follow the package directions.

A cooked loaf sounds hollow when tapped underneath—tap it firmly on the bottom with your knuckles to check.

Kneading dough

There are several methods of kneading dough, but this is a useful basic method for most types of dough:

1 Turn out the dough onto a lightly floured counter. Fold the dough in half toward you, then use the heel of your hand to push it firmly down and away from you.

2 Give the dough a quarter turn, then repeat the folding and pushing action repeatedly for about 5 minutes, until the dough is smooth and no longer sticky.

Alternatively, use a dough hook on an electric mixer or food processor; you'll need a mixer with a powerful motor for large batches of dough.

EVERYDAY CAKES

SPONGE LAYER CAKE

Preheat the oven to 350°F/180°C, then grease and line the bottoms of two 8-inch/20-cm round layer cake pans.

Sift the flour and baking powder into a bowl and add the butter, superfine sugar, and eggs. Mix together, then beat well until smooth.

Divide the mixture evenly between the prepared pans and smooth the surfaces. Bake in the preheated oven for 25–30 minutes, or until well risen and golden brown, and the cakes feel springy when lightly pressed.

Let cool in the pans for 5 minutes, then turn out and peel off the lining paper. Transfer to wire racks to cool completely. Join the cakes together with the raspberry jam, whipped heavy cream, and strawberry halves. Dust with confectioners' sugar and serve.

SERVES 8

1¼ cups self-rising flour

1 tsp baking powder

¾ cup butter, softened,
plus extra for greasing

scant 1 cup superfine sugar

3 eggs

confectioners' sugar, for dusting

filling

3 tbsp raspberry jam

1¼ cups heavy cream, whipped

16 fresh strawberries, halved

CHOCOLATE FUDGE CAKE

Grease and line the bottoms of two 8-inch/20-cm round layer cake pans.

To make the frosting, place the chocolate, brown sugar, butter, evaporated milk, and vanilla extract in a heavy-bottom pan. Heat gently, stirring continuously, until melted. Pour into a bowl and let cool. Cover and let chill in the refrigerator for 1 hour, or until spreadable.

Preheat the oven to 350°F/180°C. Place the butter and superfine sugar in a bowl and beat together until light and fluffy. Gradually beat in the eggs. Stir in the corn syrup and ground almonds. Sift the flour, salt, and cocoa into a separate bowl, then fold into the cake batter. Add a little water, if necessary, to make a dropping consistency.

Spoon the cake batter into the prepared pans and bake in the preheated oven for 30–35 minutes, or until springy to the touch and a skewer inserted in the center comes out clean.

Let stand in the pans for 5 minutes, then turn out onto wire racks to cool completely. When the cakes have cooled, sandwich them together with half the frosting. Spread the remaining frosting over the top and sides of the cake, swirling it to give a frosted appearance.

SERVES 8

¾ cup butter, softened, plus extra for greasing

generous 1 cup superfine sugar

3 eggs, beaten

3 tbsp dark corn syrup

3 tbsp ground almonds

generous 1 cup self-rising flour

pinch of salt

¼ cup unsweetened cocoa

frosting

8 oz/225 g semisweet chocolate, broken into pieces

¼ cup dark brown sugar

1 cup butter, diced

5 tbsp evaporated milk

½ tsp vanilla extract

COFFEE & WALNUT CAKE

SERVES 8

¾ cup butter, plus extra
   for greasing

¾ cup light brown sugar

3 extra-large eggs, beaten

3 tbsp strong black coffee

1½ cups self-rising flour

1½ tsp baking powder

1 cup walnut pieces

walnut halves, to decorate

frosting

½ cup butter

1¾ cups confectioners' sugar

1 tbsp strong black coffee

½ tsp vanilla extract

Preheat the oven to 350°F/180°C. Grease and line the bottoms of two 8-inch/20-cm round layer cake pans.

Cream together the butter and brown sugar until pale and fluffy. Gradually add the eggs, beating well after each addition. Beat in the coffee.

Sift the flour and baking powder into the mixture, then fold in lightly and evenly with a metal spoon. Fold in the walnut pieces.

Divide the batter between the prepared cake pans and smooth level. Bake in the preheated oven for 20–25 minutes, or until golden brown and springy to the touch. Turn out onto a wire rack to cool.

For the frosting, beat together the butter, confectioners' sugar, coffee, and vanilla extract, mixing until smooth and creamy.

Use about half of the frosting to sandwich the cakes together, then spread the remaining frosting on top and swirl with a metal spatula. Decorate with walnut halves.

TOFFEE CAKE

Preheat the oven to 350°F/180°C. Grease and line an 8-inch/20-cm square cake pan.

Put the chopped dates into a small saucepan with the boiling water and baking soda. Heat gently for about 5 minutes, without boiling, until the dates are soft.

Cream together the butter and superfine sugar in a bowl until light and fluffy. Beat in the egg, vanilla extract, and date mixture.

Fold in the flour using a metal spoon, mixing evenly. Pour the batter into the prepared cake pan. Bake in the preheated oven for 40–45 minutes, or until firm to the touch and just starting to shrink away from sides of pan.

For the toffee sauce, combine the brown sugar, butter, and cream in a saucepan and heat gently until melted. Simmer gently, stirring, for about 2 minutes.

Remove the cake from the oven and prick all over the surface with a skewer or fork. Pour the hot toffee sauce evenly over the surface. Let cool in the pan, then cut into squares.

SERVES 9

1 cup chopped pitted dried dates

¾ cup boiling water

½ tsp baking soda

6 tbsp butter, plus extra for greasing

¾ cup superfine sugar

1 extra-large egg, beaten

½ tsp vanilla extract

1½ cups self-rising flour

toffee sauce

⅓ cup light brown sugar

3 tbsp butter

2 tbsp light cream or milk

POUND CAKE

Preheat the oven to 325°F/160°C. Grease and line a 7-inch/18-cm round deep cake pan.

Cream together the butter and sugar until pale and fluffy. Add the lemon rind and gradually beat in the eggs. Sift in the flours and fold in evenly, adding enough brandy to make a soft consistency.

Spoon the batter into the prepared pan and smooth the surface. Lay the slices of citron peel on top of the cake.

Bake in the preheated oven for 1–1¼ hours, or until well risen, golden brown, and springy to the touch.

Cool in the pan for 10 minutes, then turn out and cool completely on a wire rack.

SERVES 8–10

¾ cup unsalted butter, plus extra
   for greasing

scant 1 cup superfine sugar

finely grated rind of 1 lemon

3 extra-large eggs, beaten

1 cup all-purpose flour

1 cup self-rising flour

2–3 tbsp brandy or milk

2 slices of citron peel

CLASSIC CHERRY CAKE

SERVES 8

generous 1 cup candied cherries, quartered

¾ cup ground almonds

1¾ cups all-purpose flour

1 tsp baking powder

scant 1 cup butter, plus extra for greasing

1 cup superfine sugar

3 extra-large eggs

finely grated rind and juice of 1 lemon

6 sugar cubes, crushed

Preheat the oven to 350°F/180°C. Grease an 8-inch/20-cm round cake pan and line the bottom and sides with nonstick parchment paper.

Stir together the candied cherries, ground almonds, and 1 tablespoon of the flour. Sift the remaining flour into a separate bowl with the baking powder.

Cream together the butter and sugar until light in color and fluffy in texture. Gradually add the eggs, beating hard with each addition, until evenly mixed.

Add the flour mixture and fold lightly and evenly into the creamed mixture with a metal spoon. Add the cherry mixture and fold in evenly. Finally, fold in the lemon rind and juice.

Spoon the batter into the prepared cake pan and sprinkle with the crushed sugar cubes. Bake in the preheated oven for 1–1¼ hours, or until risen, golden brown, and the cake is just beginning to shrink away from the sides of the pan.

Cool in the pan for about 15 minutes, then turn out to finish cooling on a wire rack.

FROSTED CARROT CAKE

Preheat the oven to 350°F/180°C. Grease and line the bottom of a 9-inch/23-cm square cake pan.

In a large bowl, beat the oil, brown sugar, and eggs together. Stir in the carrots, golden raisins, walnuts, and orange rind.

Sift together the flour, baking soda, cinnamon, and nutmeg, then stir evenly into the carrot mixture.

Spoon the batter into the prepared cake pan and bake in the preheated oven for 40–45 minutes, until well risen and firm to the touch.

Remove the cake from the oven and set on a wire rack for 5 minutes. Turn out onto the wire rack to cool completely.

For the frosting, combine the cream cheese, confectioners' sugar, and orange juice in a bowl and beat until smooth. Spread over the cake and swirl with a spatula. Decorate with strips of orange zest and serve cut into squares.

SERVES 16

¾ cup sunflower oil, plus extra
  for greasing

¾ cup light brown sugar

3 eggs, beaten

1¼ cups grated carrots

⅔ cup golden raisins

½ cup walnut pieces

grated rind of 1 orange

1½ cups self-rising flour

1 tsp baking soda

1 tsp ground cinnamon

½ tsp grated nutmeg

strips of orange zest, to decorate

frosting

scant 1 cup cream cheese

scant 1 cup confectioners' sugar

2 tsp orange juice

GINGERBREAD

Preheat the oven to 350°F/180°C. Grease a 9-inch/23-cm square deep cake pan and line the bottom with nonstick parchment paper.

Place the butter, sugar, and corn syrup in a saucepan and heat gently, stirring until melted. Remove from the heat.

Beat in the orange rind and juice, eggs, flours, and ground ginger, then beat thoroughly to mix evenly. Stir in the chopped candied ginger.

Spoon the batter into the prepared pan and bake in the preheated oven for 40–45 minutes, or until risen and firm to the touch.

Cool in the pan for about 10 minutes, then turn out and finish cooling on a wire rack. Cut into squares and decorate with pieces of candied ginger.

SERVES 9

¾ cup butter, plus extra for greasing

generous ⅔ cup dark brown sugar

¾ cup dark corn syrup

finely grated rind and juice of 1 small orange

2 extra-large eggs, beaten

2 cups self-rising flour

scant ½ cup whole wheat flour

2 tsp ground ginger

3 tbsp chopped candied ginger or preserved ginger

pieces of candied ginger or preserved ginger, to decorate

CARIBBEAN COCONUT CAKE

SERVES 10

1¼ cups butter, softened, plus extra for greasing

scant 1 cup superfine sugar

3 eggs

1¼ cups self-rising flour

1½ tsp baking powder

½ tsp freshly grated nutmeg

⅔ cup dry unsweetened coconut

5 tbsp coconut cream

2¾ cups confectioners' sugar

5 tbsp pineapple jam

toasted dry unsweetened coconut, to decorate

Preheat the oven to 350°F/180°C. Grease and line the bottoms of two 8-inch/20-cm round layer cake pans.

Place ¾ cup of the butter in a bowl with the superfine sugar and eggs and sift in the flour, baking powder, and nutmeg. Beat together until smooth, then stir in the coconut and 2 tablespoons of the coconut cream.

Divide the batter between the prepared pans and smooth the surfaces. Bake in the preheated oven for 25 minutes, or until golden and firm to the touch. Let cool in the pans for 5 minutes, then turn out onto a wire rack, peel off the lining paper, and let cool completely.

Sift the confectioners' sugar into a bowl and add the remaining butter and coconut cream. Beat together until smooth. Spread the pineapple jam on one of the cakes and top with just under half of the buttercream. Place the other cake on top. Spread the remaining buttercream on top of the cake and scatter with the toasted coconut.

DEVIL'S FOOD CAKE

Preheat the oven to 325°F/160°C. Grease and line the bottoms of two 8-inch/20-cm round layer cake pans.

Break up the chocolate and place with the milk and cocoa in a heatproof bowl set over over a saucepan of gently simmering water, stirring until melted and smooth. Remove from the heat.

In a large bowl, beat together the butter and brown sugar until pale and fluffy. Beat in the egg yolks, then the sour cream and melted chocolate mixture. Sift in the flour and baking soda, then fold in evenly. In a separate bowl, whip the egg whites until stiff enough to hold firm peaks. Fold into the mixture lightly and evenly.

Divide the batter between the prepared cake pans, smooth the surfaces, and bake in the preheated oven for 35–40 minutes, or until risen and firm to the touch. Cool in the pans for 10 minutes, then turn out onto a wire rack.

For the frosting, place the chocolate, cocoa, sour cream, corn syrup, butter, and water in a saucepan and heat gently without boiling, until melted. Remove from the heat and add the confectioners' sugar, stirring until smooth. Cool, stirring occasionally, until the mixture begins to thicken and hold its shape.

Split the cakes in half horizontally with a sharp knife to make four layers. Sandwich the cakes together with about a third of the frosting. Spread the remainder over the top and sides of the cakes, swirling with a spatula.

SERVES 8–10

5 oz/140 g semisweet chocolate

scant ½ cup milk

2 tbsp unsweetened cocoa

⅔ cup butter, plus extra
  for greasing

⅔ cup light brown sugar

3 eggs, separated

4 tbsp sour cream

1¾ cups all-purpose flour

1 tsp baking soda

frosting

5 oz/140 g semisweet chocolate

⅓ cup unsweetened cocoa

4 tbsp sour cream

1 tbsp dark corn syrup

3 tbsp butter

4 tbsp water

1¾ cups confectioners' sugar

ANGEL FOOD CAKE

Preheat the oven to 325°F/160°C. Brush the inside of a 7½-cup angel cake pan with oil and dust lightly with flour.

In a large grease-free bowl, whisk the egg whites until they hold soft peaks. Add the cream of tartar and whisk again until the whites are stiff but not dry.

Whisk in the almond extract, then add the sugar a tablespoon at a time, whisking hard between each addition. Sift in the flour and fold in lightly and evenly using a large metal spoon.

Spoon the batter into the prepared cake pan and tap on the counter to remove any large air bubbles. Bake in the preheated oven for 40–45 minutes, or until golden brown and firm to the touch.

Run the tip of a small knife around the edge of the cake to loosen from the pan. Let cool in the pan for 10 minutes, then turn out onto a wire rack to finish cooling.

To serve, place the berries, lemon juice, and confectioners' sugar in a saucepan and heat gently until the sugar has dissolved. Serve with the cake.

SERVES 10

sunflower oil, for greasing

8 extra-large egg whites

1 tsp cream of tartar

1 tsp almond extract

1¼ cups superfine sugar

1 cup all-purpose flour, plus extra for dusting

to serve

2¼ cups berries, such as strawberries and raspberries

1 tbsp lemon juice

2 tbsp confectioners' sugar

RICH FRUITCAKE

SERVES 16

scant 2½ cups golden raisins

1⅔ cups raisins

½ cup chopped plumped dried apricots

½ cup chopped pitted dates

4 tbsp dark rum or brandy, plus extra for flavoring (optional)

finely grated rind and juice of 1 orange

1 cup butter, plus extra for greasing

1 cup light brown sugar

4 eggs

generous ⅓ cup chopped candied peel

⅓ cup candied cherries, quartered

2 tbsp chopped candied ginger or preserved ginger

⅓ cup chopped blanched almonds

1¾ cups all-purpose flour

1 tsp apple pie spice

Place the golden raisins, raisins, apricots, and dates in a large bowl and stir in the rum, orange rind, and orange juice. Cover and let soak for several hours or overnight.

Preheat the oven to 300°F/150°C. Grease and line an 8-inch/20-cm round deep cake pan.

Cream together the butter and sugar until light and fluffy. Gradually beat in the eggs, beating hard after each addition. Stir in the soaked fruits, candied peel, candied cherries, candied ginger, and blanched almonds.

Sift together the flour and apple pie spice, then fold lightly and evenly into the mixture. Spoon into the prepared cake pan and level the surface, making a slight depression in the center with the back of the spoon.

Bake in the preheated oven for 2¼–2¾ hours, or until the cake is beginning to shrink away from the sides of the pan and a toothpick inserted into the center comes out clean. Cool completely in the pan.

Turn out the cake and remove the lining paper. Wrap with wax paper and foil and store for at least 2 months before use. To add a richer flavor, prick the cake with a toothpick and spoon over a couple of tablespoons of rum or brandy, if using, before storing.

CRISPY-TOPPED FRUIT LOAF

Preheat the oven to 375°F/190°C. Grease and line a 9 x 5 x 3-inch/ 23 x 13 x 8-cm loaf pan.

Peel, core, and finely dice the apples. Place them in a saucepan with the lemon juice, bring to a boil, cover, and simmer for about 10 minutes, until soft and pulpy. Beat well and set aside to cool.

Sift the flour, baking powder, and cinnamon into a bowl, adding any husks that remain in the sifter. Stir in ½ cup of the blackberries and the sugar.

Make a well in the center of the ingredients and add the egg, yogurt, and cooled apple puree. Mix well to incorporate thoroughly.

Spoon the batter into the prepared pan and smooth the top. Sprinkle with the remaining blackberries, pressing them down into the cake batter, and top with the crushed sugar cubes. Bake in the preheated oven for 40–45 minutes. Remove from the oven and set aside in the pan to cool.

Remove the loaf from the pan and peel away the lining paper. Serve dusted with cinnamon.

SERVES 10

butter, for greasing

12 oz/350 g baking apples

3 tbsp lemon juice

2½ cups self-rising whole wheat flour

½ tsp baking powder

1 tsp ground cinnamon, plus extra for dusting

¾ cup prepared blackberries, thawed if frozen

¾ cup light brown sugar

1 egg, beaten

scant 1 cup low-fat plain yogurt

2 oz/55 g white or brown sugar cubes, lightly crushed

CHOCOLATE & VANILLA MARBLED LOAF

Preheat the oven to 325°F/160°C. Grease a 8 x 4 x 2-inch/ 20 x 10 x 5-cm loaf pan and line the bottom with nonstick parchment paper. Dust a little flour around the inside of the pan, shaking out the excess.

Break up the chocolate, place it in a small heatproof bowl with the milk, and set the bowl over a saucepan of simmering water. Heat gently until just melted. Remove from the heat.

Cream together the butter and sugar until light and fluffy. Beat in the egg and sour cream. Sift the flour and baking powder over the mixture, then fold in lightly and evenly using a metal spoon.

Spoon half the batter into a separate bowl and stir in the chocolate mixture. Add the vanilla extract to the plain batter.

Spoon the chocolate and vanilla batters alternately into the prepared loaf pan, swirling lightly with a knife or skewer for a marbled effect. Bake in the preheated oven for 40–45 minutes, or until well risen and firm to the touch.

Cool in the pan for 10 minutes, then turn out and finish cooling on a wire rack.

SERVES 8

2 oz/55 g semisweet chocolate

3 tbsp milk

5 tbsp butter, plus extra for greasing

scant ½ cup superfine sugar

1 egg, beaten

3 tbsp sour cream

1 cup self-rising flour, plus extra for dusting

½ tsp baking powder

½ tsp vanilla extract

BANANA LOAF

SERVES 8

butter, for greasing

scant 1 cup white self-rising flour

scant ¾ cup light brown self-rising flour

generous ¾ cup raw brown sugar

pinch of salt

½ tsp ground cinnamon

½ tsp ground nutmeg

2 large ripe bananas, peeled

¾ cup orange juice

2 eggs, beaten

4 tbsp canola oil

Preheat the oven to 350°F/180°C. Lightly grease and line a 9 x 5 x 3-inch/23 x 13 x 8-cm loaf pan.

Sift the flours, sugar, salt, and the spices into a large bowl. In a separate bowl, mash the bananas with the orange juice, then stir in the eggs and oil. Pour into the dry ingredients and mix well.

Spoon into the prepared loaf pan and bake in the preheated oven for 1 hour, then test to see if the loaf is cooked by inserting a skewer into the center. If it comes out clean, the loaf is done. If not, bake for an additional 10 minutes and test again.

Remove from the oven and let cool in the pan. Turn out the loaf, slice, and serve.

DATE & WALNUT LOAF

Preheat the oven to 350°F/180°C. Grease a 8 x 4 x 2-inch/
20 x 10 x 5-cm loaf pan and line the bottom with nonstick
parchment paper.

Place the dates, baking soda, and lemon rind in a bowl and add
the hot tea. Let soak for 10 minutes, until softened.

Cream together the butter and sugar until light and fluffy, then
beat in the egg. Stir in the date mixture.

Fold in the flour using a large metal spoon, then fold in the
chopped walnuts. Spoon the mixture into the prepared cake pan
and spread evenly. Top with walnut halves.

Bake in the preheated oven for 35–40 minutes, or until risen,
firm, and golden brown. Cool for 10 minutes in the pan, then turn
out the loaf and finish cooling on a wire rack.

SERVES 8

generous ½ cup chopped pitted
dates

½ tsp baking soda

finely grated rind of ½ lemon

scant ½ cup hot tea

3 tbsp butter, plus extra
for greasing

⅓ cup light brown sugar

1 egg

generous 1 cup self-rising flour

¼ cup chopped walnuts

walnut halves, to decorate

GLOSSY FRUIT LOAF

Place the raisins, apricots, and dates in a bowl, pour over the tea, and let soak for 8 hours, or overnight.

Preheat the oven to 325°F/160°C. Grease and line a 9 x 5 x 3-inch/23 x 13 x 8-cm loaf pan.

Beat the butter and sugar together until light and fluffy. Gradually beat in the eggs, then fold in the flour alternately with the soaked fruit. Gently stir in the candied pineapple, candied cherries, and chopped Brazil nuts. Spoon the batter into the prepared pan. For the topping, arrange the walnut halves, whole Brazil nuts, and candied cherries over the surface.

Bake in the preheated oven for 1½–1¾ hours, or until a skewer inserted into the center comes out clean. Let cool in the pan for 10 minutes, then turn out and peel off the lining paper. Transfer to a wire rack to cool completely. Warm the apricot jam and brush over the top of the cake.

SERVES 10

⅓ cup raisins

½ cup plumped dried apricots, coarsely chopped

⅓ cup chopped pitted dates

⅓ cup cold black tea

½ cup butter, plus extra for greasing

generous ½ cup light brown sugar

2 eggs, beaten

1¼ cups self-rising flour, sifted

scant ⅓ cup coarsely chopped candied pineapple

scant ½ cup candied cherries, halved

generous ½ cup coarsely chopped Brazil nuts

topping

walnut halves

whole Brazil nuts

candied cherries, halved

2 tbsp apricot jam, strained

CHECKERBOARD SPONGE CAKE

SERVES 6–8

½ cup butter or margarine, softened, plus extra for greasing

generous ½ cup superfine sugar, plus extra for sprinkling

2 eggs, lightly beaten

1 tsp vanilla extract

1 cup self-rising flour, sifted

a few drops of pink edible food coloring

2–3 tbsp apricot jam

10½ oz/300 g marzipan

Preheat the oven to 350°F/180°C. Grease and line a 7-inch/18-cm square shallow baking pan. Cut a strip of double parchment paper and grease it. Use this to divide the pan in half.

Cream the butter and sugar in a mixing bowl until pale and fluffy. Gently beat in the eggs and vanilla extract, gradually adding in the flour. Spoon half the batter into a separate bowl and mix in a few drops of food coloring.

Spoon the plain batter into one half of the prepared baking pan. Spoon the colored batter into the other half of the pan, making the divide as straight as possible. Bake in the preheated oven for 35–40 minutes. Turn out and let cool on a wire rack.

When cool, trim the edges and cut the cake portions lengthwise in half, making four equal parts. Warm the jam in a small saucepan. Brush two sides of each cake portion with some of the jam and stick them together to create a checkerboard effect.

Knead the marzipan with a few drops of food coloring to color it a subtle shade of pink. Roll out the marzipan to a rectangle wide enough to wrap around the cake. Brush the outside of the cake with the remaining jam. Place the cake on the marzipan and wrap the marzipan around it, making sure that the seam is on one corner of the cake. Trim the edges neatly. Crimp the top edges of the cake, if you like, and sprinkle with sugar.

LEMON CORNMEAL CAKE

Preheat the oven to 350°F/180°C. Lightly grease an 8-inch/20-cm round deep cake pan and line the bottom with parchment paper.

Beat together the butter and sugar until pale and fluffy. Beat in the lemon rind, lemon juice, eggs, and ground almonds. Sift in the cornmeal and baking powder and stir until evenly mixed.

Spoon the batter into the prepared pan and spread evenly. Bake in the preheated oven for 30–35 minutes, or until just firm to the touch and golden brown. Remove the cake from the oven and cool in the pan for 20 minutes.

For the syrup, place the lemon juice, sugar, and water in a small saucepan. Heat gently, stirring until the sugar has dissolved, then bring to a boil and simmer for 3–4 minutes, or until slightly reduced and syrupy.

Turn out the cake onto a wire rack, then drizzle half of the syrup evenly over the surface. Let cool completely.

Cut the cake into slices, drizzle the extra syrup over the top, and serve with sour cream.

SERVES 8

scant 1 cup unsalted butter, plus extra for greasing

1 cup superfine sugar

finely grated rind and juice of 1 large lemon

3 eggs, beaten

1¼ cups ground almonds

scant ¾ cup quick-cook cornmeal

1 tsp baking powder

sour cream, to serve

syrup

juice of 2 lemons

¼ cup superfine sugar

2 tbsp water

APPLE CAKE WITH STREUSEL TOPPING

Preheat the oven to 350°F/180°C. Grease an 8-inch/20-cm round loose-bottom cake pan and line the bottom with parchment paper. Toss the apples in the lemon juice.

Cream together the butter and superfine sugar until pale and fluffy, then gradually add the eggs, beating thoroughly after each addition. Sift together the flour, baking powder, cinnamon, and nutmeg into the mixture and fold in lightly and evenly using a metal spoon. Stir in the hard cider.

Stir the apples into the batter to distribute evenly, then spoon into the prepared pan and level the surface.

For the streusel topping, combine the hazelnuts, flour, brown sugar, and cinnamon, then stir in the melted butter, mixing until crumbly. Spread over the cake.

Bake the cake in the preheated oven for 1–1¼ hours, or until firm and golden brown. Cool for 10 minutes in the pan, then remove carefully and finish cooling on a wire rack.

SERVES 8

1 lb 2 oz/500 g apples, peeled, cored, and cut into ½-inch/ 1-cm dice

1 tbsp lemon juice

generous ½ cup unsalted butter, plus extra for greasing

⅔ cup superfine sugar

2 extra-large eggs, beaten

2 cups all-purpose flour

3 tsp baking powder

1 tsp ground cinnamon

½ tsp ground nutmeg

3 tbsp hard cider or apple juice

streusel topping

⅓ cup hazelnuts, skinned and finely chopped

⅓ cup all-purpose flour

2 tbsp light brown sugar

½ tsp ground cinnamon

2 tbsp unsalted butter, melted

HONEY & ALMOND CAKE

SERVES 12–16

generous ⅔ cup unsalted butter, plus extra for greasing

½ cup light brown sugar

¾ cup honey

1 tbsp lemon juice

2 eggs, beaten

1¾ cups self-rising flour

1 tbsp slivered almonds

warmed honey, to glaze

Preheat the oven to 350°F/180°C. Grease an 8-inch/20-cm square deep cake pan and line the bottom with parchment paper.

Put the butter, sugar, honey, and lemon juice in a saucepan and stir over medium heat, without boiling, until melted and smooth. Remove the pan from the heat and quickly beat in the eggs with a wooden spoon. Sift in the flour and stir lightly and evenly with a metal spoon.

Pour the batter into the prepared pan and sprinkle the slivered almonds over the top. Bake in the preheated oven for 35–40 minutes, until risen, firm, and golden brown.

Let cool in the pan for about 15 minutes, then turn out and cool completely on a wire rack. Brush with warmed honey and cut into slices to serve.

EVERYDAY CAKES

PINEAPPLE UPSIDE-DOWN CAKE

Preheat the oven to 325°F/160°C. Grease a 9-inch/23-cm round deep cake pan with a solid bottom and line the bottom with parchment paper.

For the topping, place the butter and corn syrup in a heavy-bottom pan and heat gently until melted. Bring to a boil and boil for 2–3 minutes, stirring, until slightly thickened and taffylike.

Pour the syrup into the bottom of the prepared pan. Arrange the pineapple rings and candied cherries in a single layer over the syrup.

Place the eggs, sugar, and vanilla extract in a large heatproof bowl set over a saucepan of gently simmering water and whisk with an electric mixer for 10–15 minutes, until thick enough to leave a trail when the whisk is lifted. Sift in the flour and baking powder and fold in lightly and evenly with a metal spoon.

Fold the melted butter into the mixture with a metal spoon until evenly mixed. Spoon into the prepared pan and bake in the preheated oven for 1–1¼ hours, or until well risen, firm, and golden brown.

Let cool in the pan for 10 minutes, then carefully turn out onto a serving plate. Serve warm or cold.

SERVES 10

4 eggs, beaten

1 cup superfine sugar

1 tsp vanilla extract

1¾ cups all-purpose flour

2 tsp baking powder

generous ½ cup unsalted butter, melted, plus extra for greasing

topping

3 tbsp unsalted butter

4 tbsp dark corn syrup

15 oz/425 g canned pineapple rings, drained

4–6 candied cherries, halved

ORANGE & POPPY SEED BUNDT CAKE

Preheat the oven to 325°F/160°C. Grease and lightly flour a Bundt ring pan, about 9½ inches/24 cm in diameter and with a capacity of approximately 8¾ cups.

Cream together the butter and sugar until pale and fluffy, then add the eggs gradually, beating thoroughly after each addition. Stir in the orange rind and poppy seeds. Sift in the flour and baking powder, then fold in evenly.

Add the milk and orange juice, stirring to mix evenly. Spoon the batter into the prepared pan and bake in the preheated oven for 45–50 minutes, or until firm and golden brown. Cool in the pan for 10 minutes, then turn out onto a wire rack to cool.

For the syrup, place the sugar and orange juice in a saucepan and heat gently until the sugar melts. Bring to a boil and simmer for about 5 minutes, until reduced and syrupy.

Spoon the syrup over the cake while it is still warm. Top with the strips of orange zest and serve warm or cold.

SERVES 10

scant 1 cup unsalted butter, plus extra for greasing

1 cup superfine sugar

3 extra-large eggs, beaten

finely grated rind of 1 orange

¼ cup poppy seeds

2¼ cups all-purpose flour, plus extra for dusting

2 tsp baking powder

⅔ cup milk

½ cup orange juice

strips of orange zest, to decorate

syrup

scant ¾ cup superfine sugar

⅔ cup orange juice

CELEBRATION CAKES

BIRTHDAY LEMON SPONGE CAKE

Preheat the oven to 350°F/180°C. Grease two 8-inch/20-cm layer cake pans and line the bottoms with parchment paper.

Cream together the butter and superfine sugar until pale and fluffy. Gradually add the eggs, beating well after each addition. Sift in the flour and fold in evenly with a metal spoon. Fold in the lemon rind and milk lightly and evenly.

Spoon the batter into the prepared pans and bake in the preheated oven for 25–30 minutes, or until golden brown and springy to the touch. Let the cakes cool in the pans for 2–3 minutes, then turn out onto a wire rack to finish cooling.

For the butter frosting, beat together the butter, confectioners' sugar, and lemon juice until smooth. Mix about 3 tablespoons of the butter cream with the lemon curd. Use the lemon curd mixture to sandwich together the two cakes.

Spread about two thirds of the remaining butter frosting over the top of the cake, swirling with a spatula. Spoon the remainder into a pastry bag and pipe swirls around the edge of the cake. Add candleholders and birthday candles to finish.

SERVES 8–10

sponge
generous 1 cup unsalted butter, plus extra for greasing

1¼ cups superfine sugar

4 eggs, beaten

2¼ cups self-rising flour

finely grated rind of 1 lemon

3 tbsp milk

butter frosting
⅔ cup unsalted butter

1¾ cups confectioners' sugar

2 tbsp lemon juice or lemon liqueur (Limoncello)

3 tbsp lemon curd

DOTTY CHOCOLATE CHIP CAKE

Preheat the oven to 325°F/170°C. Grease an 8-inch/20-cm round cake pan and line the bottom with parchment paper.

Place the margarine, sugar, eggs, flour, baking powder, and cocoa in a bowl and beat until just smooth. Stir in the chocolate chips, mixing evenly.

Spoon the batter into the prepared pan and spread the top level. Bake in the preheated oven for 40–45 minutes, until risen and firm to the touch. Cool in the pan for 5 minutes, then turn out and finish cooling completely on a wire rack.

For the frosting, place the chocolate, butter, and corn syrup in a saucepan over low heat and stir until just melted and smooth.

Remove from the heat and let cool until it begins to thicken enough to leave a trail when the spoon is lifted. Pour the frosting over the top of the cake, letting it drizzle down the sides. Arrange the candies over the top of the cake.

SERVES 10

¾ cup soft margarine or softened butter, plus extra for greasing

scant 1 cup superfine sugar

3 eggs, beaten

1½ cups all-purpose flour

1½ tsp baking powder

2 tbsp unsweetened cocoa

⅓ cup white chocolate chips

topping

6 oz/175 g milk chocolate or semisweet chocolate

scant ½ cup unsalted butter or margarine

1 tbsp dark corn syrup

1½ oz/40 g small colored candies

CELEBRATION CAKES

70

VALENTINE CHOCOLATE HEART CAKE

SERVES 12

1½ cups self-rising flour

2 tsp baking powder

½ cup unsweetened cocoa

3 eggs

scant ¾ cup light brown sugar

⅔ cup sunflower oil, plus extra for greasing

⅔ cup light cream

fresh mint sprigs, to decorate

filling and topping

8 oz/225 g semisweet chocolate

generous 1 cup heavy cream

3 tbsp seedless raspberry jam

generous 1 cup fresh or frozen raspberries

Preheat the oven to 350°F/180°C. Grease an 8 inch/20 cm wide heart-shape cake pan and line the bottom with parchment paper.

Sift the flour, baking powder, and cocoa into a large bowl. Beat the eggs with the sugar, oil, and light cream. Make a well in the dry ingredients and add the egg mixture, then stir to mix thoroughly, beating to a smooth batter.

Pour the batter into the prepared pan and bake in the preheated oven for 25–30 minutes, or until risen and firm to the touch. Cool in the pan for 10 minutes, then turn out and finish cooling on a wire rack.

For the filling and topping, place the chocolate and heavy cream in a saucepan over low heat and stir until melted. Remove from the heat and stir until the mixture cools slightly and begins to thicken.

Use a sharp knife to cut the cake in half horizontally. Spread the cut surface of each half with the raspberry jam, then top with about 3 tablespoons of the chocolate mixture. Sprinkle over half the raspberries and replace the top, pressing down lightly.

Spread the remaining chocolate mixture over the top and sides of the cake, swirling with a spatula. Top with the remaining raspberries and decorate with mint sprigs.

EASTER MARZIPAN FRUITCAKE

Preheat the oven to 300°F/150°C. Grease and line an 8-inch/20-cm round deep cake pan with parchment paper.

Place the butter and sugar in a bowl and cream together with an electric whisk or wooden spoon until pale, light, and fluffy. Gradually beat in the eggs, beating hard after each addition.

Sift together the flour, baking powder, and apple pie spice. Use a large metal spoon to fold into the creamed mixture. Stir in the lemon rind, currants, golden raisins, and candied peel, mixing evenly. Spoon half the batter into the prepared pan and smooth level.

Roll out 9 oz/250 g of the marzipan to an 8-inch/20-cm round and place over the batter in the pan. Add the remaining cake batter and smooth level. Bake the cake in the preheated oven for 2¼–2¾ hours, or until firm and golden and the sides are beginning to shrink away from the pan. Let cool in the pan for 30 minutes, then turn out onto a wire rack to finish cooling.

Brush the top of the cake with apricot jam. Roll out two thirds of the remaining marzipan to a round to cover the top of the cake. Use a knife to mark a lattice design in the surface and pinch the edges to decorate.

Roll the remaining marzipan into eleven small balls and arrange around the edge of the cake. Place under a hot broiler for 30–40 seconds to brown lightly. Cool before storing.

SERVES 16

¾ cup unsalted butter, plus extra for greasing

scant 1 cup light brown sugar

3 eggs, beaten

2 cups all-purpose flour

½ tsp baking powder

2 tsp apple pie spice

finely grated rind of 1 small lemon

scant ½ cup currants

scant ¾ cup golden raisins

⅓ cup chopped candied peel

1 lb 9 oz/700 g marzipan

3 tbsp apricot jam

EASTER CUPCAKES

Preheat the oven to 350°F/180°C. Place 12 paper liners into a shallow muffin pan.

Put the butter and sugar in a bowl and beat together until light and fluffy. Gradually add the eggs, beating well after each addition. Sift in the flour and cocoa and, using a large metal spoon, fold into the mixture. Spoon the batter into the paper liners.

Bake in the preheated oven for 15–20 minutes, or until well risen and firm to the touch. Transfer to a wire rack and let cool.

To make the buttercream frosting, put the butter in a bowl and beat until fluffy. Sift in the confectioners' sugar and beat together until well mixed, adding the milk and vanilla extract.

When the cupcakes are cold, put the frosting in a pastry bag fitted with a large star tip, and pipe a circle around the edge of each cupcake to form a nest. Place chocolate eggs in the center of each nest to decorate.

MAKES 12

8 tbsp butter, softened, or soft margarine

generous ½ cup superfine sugar

2 eggs, lightly beaten

generous ½ cup self-rising flour

generous ¼ cup unsweetened cocoa

topping

6 tbsp butter, softened

1½ cups confectioners' sugar

1 tbsp milk

2–3 drops of vanilla extract

9 oz/250 g mini candy shell chocolate eggs

ROSE-TOPPED WEDDING MUFFINS

MAKES 12

oil or melted butter, for greasing (optional)

2 cups all-purpose flour

1 tbsp baking powder

⅛ tsp salt

generous ½ cup superfine sugar

2 large eggs

1 cup milk

6 tbsp sunflower oil or melted, cooled butter

1 tsp vanilla extract

12 store-bought sugar roses or fresh rose petals or buds, to decorate

frosting

1½ cups confectioners' sugar

3–4 tsp hot water

Preheat the oven to 400°F/200°C. Increase the quantity of ingredients according to the number of wedding guests invited, working in double quantities to make 24 muffins each time. Grease the appropriate number of muffin pans or line with muffin paper liners.

Sift together the flour, baking powder, and salt into a large bowl. Stir in the superfine sugar.

Lightly beat the eggs in a large pitcher or bowl, then beat in the milk, oil, and vanilla extract. Make a well in the center of the dry ingredients and pour in the beaten liquid ingredients. Stir gently until just combined; do not overmix.

Spoon the batter into the prepared muffin pans. Bake in the preheated oven for about 20 minutes, until well risen, golden brown, and firm to the touch.

Let the muffins cool in the pans for 5 minutes, then transfer to a wire rack and let cool completely. Store the muffins in the freezer until required.

On the day of serving, if using fresh flowers, rinse and let dry on paper towels. For the frosting, sift the confectioners' sugar into a bowl. Add the water and stir until the mixture is smooth and thick enough to coat the back of a wooden spoon. Spoon the frosting on top of each muffin, then top with a sugar rose, rose petal, or rose bud.

HALLOWEEN SPIDERWEB CAKE

Preheat the oven to 325°F/170°C. Grease a 7-inch/18-cm round cake pan and line the bottom with parchment paper.

Cream together the butter and superfine sugar until light and fluffy. Beat in the eggs and milk. Sift in the flour and baking powder, then fold in lightly and evenly using a metal spoon.

Spoon half the batter into a separate bowl and stir in a few drops of orange food coloring, stirring to mix evenly. Place alternate spoonfuls of the plain and orange batters into the prepared cake pan, swirling lightly for a marbled effect. Bake in the preheated oven for 35–40 minutes, or until well-risen and firm to the touch. Cool in the pan for 10 minutes, then turn out and finish cooling on a wire rack.

Reserve about 1½ oz/40 g of the fondant and color it black with food coloring, then color the remaining fondant with orange food coloring. Place the cake on a board or plate and brush the top and sides with apricot jam. Roll out the orange fondant on a counter lightly dusted with confectioner's sugar so that it is large enough to cover the cake, then lift it onto the cake, smoothing with your hands. Trim the edges at the bottom, reserving the trimmings.

Place the confectioners' sugar in a small bowl and stir in enough water to mix to a paste, adding a few drops of black food coloring. Spoon into a small pastry bag fitted with a medium plain tip, then pipe a spiderweb design over the top of the cake. Shape about half of the black fondant into an oval for the spider's body, then shape eight legs from the remaining black fondant. Shape two eyes from the orange fondant trimmings. Place on the web.

SERVES 8–10

- ½ cup unsalted butter, plus extra for greasing
- generous ½ cup superfine sugar
- 2 eggs, beaten
- 3 tbsp milk
- 1¼ cups self-rising flour
- ½ tsp baking powder
- a few drops of orange edible food coloring

topping

- 1 lb 2 oz/500 g ready-to-roll fondant
- a few drops of black and orange edible food colorings
- 2 tbsp apricot jam, warmed
- scant 1 cup confectioners' sugar, plus extra for dusting

GOLDEN CHRISTMAS CAKE

Place the chopped apricots, mango, and pineapple in a bowl with the golden raisins, preserved ginger, and candied peel. Stir in the orange rind, orange juice, and brandy. Cover the bowl and let soak overnight.

Preheat the oven to 325°F/170°C. Grease a 9-inch/23-cm round springform cake pan and line with parchment paper.

Cream together the butter and brown sugar until the mixture is pale and fluffy. Add the eggs, beating well between each addition. Stir in the honey.

Sift the flour with the allspice and fold into the mixture using a metal spoon. Add the soaked fruit and pecans, stirring thoroughly to mix. Spoon the batter into the prepared pan, spreading it evenly, then make a slight dip in the center.

Place the pan in the center of the preheated oven and bake for 1½–2 hours, or until golden brown and firm to the touch and a toothpick inserted into the center comes out clean. Let cool in the pan.

Turn the cake out, remove the lining paper, and re-wrap in clean parchment paper and foil. Store in a cool place for at least 1 month before use. If you want, cover the cake with marzipan and fondant, following the package instructions, and decorate with silver dragées.

SERVES 16–18

¾ cup chopped plumped dried apricots

⅓ cup chopped plumped dried mango

⅓ cup chopped plumped dried pineapple

generous 1 cup golden raisins

¼ cup chopped preserved ginger

⅓ cup chopped candied peel

finely grated rind and juice of 1 orange

4 tbsp brandy

¾ cup unsalted butter, plus extra for greasing

½ cup light brown sugar

4 eggs, beaten

2 tbsp honey

1½ cups self-rising flour

2 tsp ground allspice

¾ cup pecans

topping (optional)

1 lb 12 oz/800 g marzipan

2 lb/900 g ready-to-roll fondant frosting

silver dragées

CHRISTMAS SNOWFLAKE MUFFINS

MAKES 12

oil or melted butter, for greasing (if using)

2 cups all-purpose flour

1 tbsp baking powder

1 tsp allspice

⅛ tsp salt

generous ½ cup firmly packed dark brown sugar

2 large eggs

scant ½ cup milk

6 tbsp sunflower oil or melted, cooled butter

⅔ cup luxury mincemeat with candied cherries and nuts

1 lb/450 g ready-to-roll frosting

confectioners' sugar, for dusting

2½ tsp apricot jam

silver dragées, to decorate

Preheat the oven to 400°F/200°C. Grease a 12-cup muffin pan or line with 12 muffin paper liners.

Sift together the flour, baking powder, allspice, and salt into a large bowl. Stir in the brown sugar.

Lightly beat the eggs in a large pitcher or bowl, then beat in the milk and oil. Make a well in the center of the dry ingredients, pour in the beaten liquid ingredients, and add the mincemeat. Stir gently until just combined; do not overmix.

Spoon the batter into the prepared muffin pan. Bake in the preheated oven for about 20 minutes, until well risen, golden brown, and firm to the touch.

Let the muffins cool in the pan for 5 minutes, then transfer to a wire rack and let cool completely.

Knead the frosting until pliable. On a surface dusted with confectioners' sugar, roll out the frosting to a thickness of ¼ inch/5 mm. Using a 3-inch/7-cm fluted cutter, cut out 12 "snowflakes."

Warm the jam until runny, then brush it over the tops of the muffins. Place a snowflake on top, then decorate with silver dragées.

ITALIAN CHRISTMAS CAKE

Preheat the oven to 300°F/150°C. Grease an 8-inch/20-cm round cake pan or loose-bottom tart pan and line the bottom with parchment paper.

Toast the almonds under the broiler until lightly browned, and then place in a bowl. Toast the hazelnuts until the skins split. Place on a dry dish towel and rub off the skins. Coarsely chop the hazelnuts and add them to the almonds, together with the candied peel.

Chop the apricots and pineapple fairly finely and add to the nuts together with the orange rind. Mix well.

Sift the flour, cocoa, and cinnamon into the nut mixture and mix together well.

Put the sugar and honey into a saucepan and heat until the sugar dissolves. Boil gently for about 5 minutes, or until the mixture thickens and starts to turn a deeper shade of brown. Quickly add to the nut mixture and mix thoroughly. Spoon into the prepared pan and smooth the top using the back of a damp spoon.

Cook in the preheated oven for 1 hour. Remove the cake from the oven and let stand in the pan until completely cool. Turn out of the pan and carefully peel off the paper. Dust with a little confectioners' sugar before serving.

SERVES 12

butter, for greasing
1 cup whole almonds, split
¾ cup hazelnuts
½ cup chopped candied peel
⅓ cup plumped dried apricots
⅓ cup candied pineapple
grated rind of 1 large orange
½ cup all-purpose flour
2 tbsp unsweetened cocoa
2 tsp ground cinnamon
½ cup superfine sugar
½ cup honey
confectioners' sugar, for dusting

STOLLEN

Put the currants, raisins, candied peel, and candied cherries in a bowl. Stir in the rum and set aside. Put the butter, milk, and superfine sugar into a saucepan and heat gently until the sugar has dissolved and the butter has just melted. Let cool slightly. Sift the flour, salt, nutmeg, and cinnamon into a bowl. Crush the cardamom seeds and add them to the flour mixture. Stir in the yeast. Make a well in the center and stir in the milk mixture, lemon rind, and egg. Beat to form a soft dough.

Turn out the dough onto a floured counter. With floured hands, knead the dough for about 5 minutes. It will be quite sticky, so add more flour if necessary. Knead the soaked fruit and slivered almonds into the dough until just combined. Place the dough in a clean, lightly oiled bowl. Cover with plastic wrap and let stand in a warm place for 1½ hours, or until doubled in size. Turn out the dough onto a floured counter and knead lightly for 1–2 minutes, then roll out to a 10-inch/25-cm square.

Roll the marzipan into a sausage shape slightly shorter than the length of the dough and place down the center. Fold one side over to cover the marzipan. Repeat with the other side, overlapping in the center. Seal the ends. Place the roll, seam-side down, on a greased baking sheet. Cover with oiled plastic wrap and let stand in a warm place until doubled in size. Preheat the oven to 375°F/190°C. Bake the stollen for 40 minutes, or until it is golden and sounds hollow when tapped underneath. Brush the hot stollen generously with melted butter and dredge heavily with confectioners' sugar. Let cool on a wire rack.

SERVES 10

½ cup currants

⅓ cup raisins

scant ¼ cup chopped candied peel

⅓ cup candied cherries, rinsed, dried, and quartered

2 tbsp dark rum

4 tbsp butter

¼ cup milk

3 tbsp superfine sugar

3¼ cups white bread flour, plus extra for dusting

½ tsp salt

½ tsp ground nutmeg

½ tsp ground cinnamon

seeds from 3 cardamom pods

2 tsp active dry yeast

finely grated rind of 1 lemon

1 egg, beaten

⅓ cup slivered almonds

oil, for greasing

6 oz/175 g marzipan

melted butter, for brushing

confectioners' sugar, for dusting

SACHERTORTE

SERVES 10

6 oz/175 g semisweet chocolate

²/₃ cup unsalted butter, plus extra for greasing

²/₃ cup superfine sugar

6 eggs, separated

1¼ cups all-purpose flour

frosting and filling

8 oz/225 g semisweet chocolate

5 tbsp strong black coffee

1 cup confectioners' sugar

6 tbsp apricot jam, warmed

Preheat the oven to 300°F/150°C. Grease and line a 9-inch/23-cm springform round cake pan.

Put the chocolate in a heatproof bowl set over a saucepan of gently simmering water until melted. In a separate bowl, beat the butter and half the sugar until pale and fluffy. Add the egg yolks and beat well. Add the melted chocolate in a thin stream, beating well. Sift the flour and fold it into the mixture. Whisk the egg whites until they stand in soft peaks. Add the remaining sugar and whisk until glossy. Fold half the egg white mixture into the chocolate mixture, then fold in the remainder.

Spoon into the prepared pan and level the top. Bake in the preheated oven for 1–1¼ hours, until a skewer inserted into the center comes out clean. Cool in the pan for 5 minutes, then transfer to a wire rack to cool completely.

To make the frosting, melt 6 oz/175 g of the chocolate and beat in the coffee until smooth. Sift in the confectioners' sugar and whisk to give a thick frosting. Halve the cake. Spread the apricot jam over the cut edges and sandwich together. Invert the cake on a wire rack. Spoon the frosting over the cake and spread to coat the top and sides. Let set for 5 minutes, letting any excess drip through the rack. Transfer to a serving plate and let set for at least 2 hours.

To decorate, melt the remaining chocolate and spoon into a small pastry bag fitted with a fine plain tip. Pipe the word "Sacher" or "Sachertorte" on the top of the cake. Let set before serving.

CHOCOLATE GANACHE CAKE

Preheat the oven to 350°F/180°C. Lightly grease and line an 8-inch/20-cm springform round cake pan with parchment paper.

Beat the butter and sugar together in a bowl until light and fluffy. Gradually add the eggs, beating well after each addition. Sift the flour and cocoa together, then fold into the cake batter. Fold in the melted chocolate.

Pour into the prepared pan and smooth the top. Bake in the preheated oven for 40 minutes, or until springy to the touch. Let the cake cool for 5 minutes in the pan, then turn out onto a wire rack and let cool completely. Cut the cooled cake into two layers.

To make the ganache, place the cream in a saucepan and bring to a boil, stirring. Add the chocolate and stir until melted. Pour into a bowl, let cool, then chill for 2 hours, or until set and firm. Whisk the mixture until light and fluffy and set aside.

Reserve one third of the ganache. Use the remainder to sandwich the cake together and spread over the cake.

Melt the confectionery coating and spread it over a large sheet of parchment paper. Let cool until just set. Cut into strips a little wider than the height of the cake. Place the strips around the edge of the cake, overlapping them slightly.

Pipe the reserved ganache in teardrops or shells to cover the top of the cake. Let chill for 1 hour before serving.

SERVES 10

- ¾ cup unsalted butter, plus extra for greasing
- ¾ cup superfine sugar
- 4 eggs, lightly beaten
- 1¾ cups self-rising flour
- 1 tbsp unsweetened cocoa
- 1¾ oz/50 g semisweet chocolate, melted
- 7 oz/200 g chocolate-flavored confectionery coating, to decorate

ganache
- 2 cups heavy cream
- 13 oz/375 g semisweet chocolate, broken into pieces

RED VELVET CAKE

Preheat the oven to 375°F/190°C. Grease two 9-inch/23-cm layer cake pans and line the bottoms with parchment paper.

Place the butter, water, and cocoa in a small saucepan and heat gently, without boiling, stirring until melted and smooth. Remove from the heat and let cool slightly.

Beat together the eggs, buttermilk, vanilla extract, and food coloring until frothy. Beat in the butter mixture. Sift together the flour, cornstarch, and baking powder, then stir quickly and evenly into the mixture with the superfine sugar.

Divide the batter between the prepared pans and bake in the preheated oven for 25–30 minutes, or until risen and firm to the touch. Cool in the pans for 3–4 minutes, then turn out and finish cooling on a wire rack.

For the frosting, beat together all the ingredients until smooth. Use about half of the frosting to sandwich the cakes together, then spread the remainder over the top, swirling with a metal spatula.

(* If you prefer not to use synthetic food coloring, this can be replaced by 4 tablespoons of beet juice: you should reduce the water quantity to 2 tablespoons. If you have an electric juicer, 1 medium beet should yield about 4 tablespoons of juice.)

SERVES 12

1 cup unsalted butter, plus extra for greasing

4 tbsp water

½ cup unsweetened cocoa

3 eggs

generous 1 cup buttermilk

2 tsp vanilla extract

2 tbsp red edible food coloring*

2½ cups all-purpose flour

½ cup cornstarch

1½ tsp baking powder

scant 1½ cups superfine sugar

frosting

generous 1 cup cream cheese

3 tbsp unsalted butter

3 tbsp superfine sugar

1 tsp vanilla extract

HUMMINGBIRD CAKE

SERVES 10

scant 1 cup sunflower oil,
  plus extra for greasing

2¼ cups all-purpose flour

1¼ cups superfine sugar

1 tsp ground cinnamon

1 tsp baking soda

3 eggs, beaten

scant 1 cup pecans, coarsely
  chopped, plus extra to decorate

1 cup mashed ripe bananas
  (about 3 bananas)

3 oz/85 g canned crushed
  pineapple (drained weight),
  plus 4 tbsp juice from the can

frosting

¾ cup cream cheese

¼ cup unsalted butter

1 tsp vanilla extract

3½ cups confectioners' sugar

Preheat the oven to 350°F/180°C. Lightly grease three 9-inch/
23-cm layer cake pans with oil and line the bottoms with
parchment paper.

Sift together the flour, superfine sugar, cinnamon, and baking
soda into a large bowl. Add the eggs, oil, pecans, bananas, and
pineapple with the juice and stir with a wooden spoon until
evenly mixed.

Divide the batter among the prepared pans, spreading it evenly.
Bake in the preheated oven for 25–30 minutes, or until golden
brown and firm to the touch.

Remove the cakes from the oven and let cool for 10 minutes in
the pans before turning out onto wire racks to cool.

For the frosting, beat together the cream cheese, butter, and
vanilla extract in a bowl until smooth. Sift in the confectioners'
sugar and mix until smooth.

Sandwich the cakes together with half of the frosting, spread
the remaining frosting over the top, then sprinkle with pecans
to decorate.

WHITE CHOCOLATE COFFEE GÂTEAU

SERVES 8–10

3 tbsp unsalted butter, plus extra for greasing

3 oz/85 g white chocolate

⅔ cup superfine sugar

4 extra-large eggs, beaten

2 tbsp very strong black coffee

1 tsp vanilla extract

generous 1 cup all-purpose flour

white chocolate curls, to decorate

frosting

6 oz/175 g white chocolate

6 tbsp unsalted butter

generous ½ cup sour cream

generous 1 cup confectioners' sugar, sifted

1 tbsp coffee liqueur or very strong black coffee

Preheat the oven to 350°F/180°C. Grease two 8-inch/20-cm layer cake pans and line the bottoms with parchment paper.

Place the butter and chocolate in a bowl set over a saucepan of hot, but not simmering, water and leave on very low heat until just melted. Stir to mix lightly, then remove from the heat.

Place the superfine sugar, eggs, coffee, and vanilla extract in a large bowl set over a saucepan of hot water and whisk hard with an electric whisk until the mixture is pale and thick enough to leave a trail when the whisk is lifted.

Remove from the heat, sift in the flour, and fold in lightly and evenly. Quickly fold in the butter and chocolate mixture, then divide the batter between the prepared pans.

Bake in the preheated oven for 25–30 minutes, until risen, golden brown, and springy to the touch. Cool in the pans for 2 minutes, then run a knife around the edges to loosen and turn out onto a wire rack to cool.

For the frosting, place the chocolate and butter in a bowl set over a saucepan of hot water and heat gently until melted. Remove from the heat, stir in the sour cream, then add the confectioners' sugar and coffee liqueur and mix until smooth. Chill the frosting for at least 30 minutes, stirring occasionally, until it becomes thick and glossy.

Use about one third of the frosting to sandwich the cakes together. Spread the remainder over the top and sides, swirling with a spatula. Arrange the chocolate curls over the top of the cake and let set.

CITRUS MOUSSE CAKE

Preheat the oven to 350°F/180°C. Grease an 8-inch/20-cm springform round cake pan and and line the bottom with parchment paper.

Beat the butter and sugar in a bowl until light and fluffy. Gradually add the eggs, beating well after each addition. Sift together the flour and cocoa and then fold into the creamed mixture. Fold in the melted chocolate.

Pour into the prepared pan and level the top. Bake in the preheated oven for 40 minutes, or until springy to the touch. Let cool for 5 minutes in the pan, then turn out onto a wire rack and let cool completely. Cut the cold cake into two layers.

To make the orange mousse, beat the egg yolks and sugar until pale, then whisk in the orange juice. Sprinkle the gelatin over the water in a small heatproof bowl and let it go spongy, then place over a saucepan of hot water and stir until dissolved. Stir into the egg yolk mixture.

Whip the cream until holding its shape. Reserve a little for decoration and fold the remainder into the mousse. Whisk the egg whites until standing in soft peaks, then fold in. Let stand in a cool place until starting to set, stirring occasionally.

Place one half of the cake in the pan. Pour in the mousse and press the second half of the cake on top. Chill until set. Transfer to a plate, then spoon teaspoonfuls of cream around the top and arrange orange segments in the center.

SERVES 12

¾ cup butter, plus extra
  for greasing

¾ cup superfine sugar

4 eggs, lightly beaten

1¾ cups self-rising flour

1 tbsp unsweetened cocoa

1¾ oz/50 g orange-flavored
  semisweet chocolate, melted

peeled orange segments,
  to decorate

mousse

2 eggs, separated

4 tbsp superfine sugar

¾ cup freshly squeezed
  orange juice

2 tsp gelatin

3 tbsp water

1¼ cups heavy cream

CHOCOLATE TRUFFLE TORTE

SERVES 10

unsalted butter, for greasing

¼ cup superfine sugar

2 eggs

¼ cup all-purpose flour

¼ cup unsweetened cocoa

4 tbsp cold, strong black coffee

2 tbsp cognac

unsweetened cocoa and
   confectioners' sugar,
   to decorate

filling

2½ cups heavy cream

15 oz/425 g semisweet chocolate,
   broken into pieces

Preheat the oven to 425°F/220°C. Grease a 9-inch/23-cm springform round cake pan and line with parchment paper.

Put the sugar and eggs in a heatproof bowl set over a saucepan of gently simmering water. Whisk together until pale and resembling the texture of mousse. Sift in the flour and cocoa and fold gently into the batter.

Pour into the prepared pan and bake in the preheated oven for 7–10 minutes, or until risen and firm to the touch. Turn the cake out of the pan and place on a wire rack to cool. Wash and dry the pan and replace the cooled cake in the pan. Mix together the coffee and cognac and brush over the cake.

To make the truffle filling, put the cream in a bowl and whisk until just holding very soft peaks. Put the chocolate in a heatproof bowl set over a saucepan of gently simmering water until melted. Let cool. Carefully fold the cooled melted chocolate into the cream. Pour the chocolate mixture over the sponge. Chill until set.

To decorate the torte, sift cocoa over the top and remove carefully from the pan. Using strips of card or wax paper, sift bands of confectioners' sugar over the torte to create a striped pattern. To serve, cut into slices with a hot knife.

RASPBERRY & CHOCOLATE MERINGUE

Preheat the oven to 275°F/140°C. Draw three rectangles, measuring 4 x 10 inches/10 x 25 cm, on sheets of parchment paper and place on two cookie sheets.

Whisk the egg whites in a mixing bowl until soft peaks form, then gradually whisk in half of the sugar and continue whisking until the mixture is very stiff and glossy.

Carefully fold in the remaining sugar, the cornstarch, and the grated chocolate with a metal spoon or a spatula.

Spoon the meringue mixture into a pastry bag fitted with a ½-inch/1-cm plain tip and pipe lines across the rectangles.

Bake in the preheated oven for 1½ hours, changing the position of the cookie sheets halfway through. Without opening the oven door, turn off the oven and let the meringues cool inside the oven, then peel away the parchment paper.

Place the chocolate in a heatproof bowl set over a saucepan of gently simmering water until melted. Spread the chocolate over two of the meringue layers. Let set.

Place one chocolate-coated meringue on a plate and top with about one third of the cream and raspberries. Gently place the second chocolate-coated meringue on top and spread with half of the remaining cream and raspberries. Place the last meringue on the top and decorate with the remaining cream and raspberries.

Drizzle the melted chocolate over the top and serve.

SERVES 10

3 egg whites

¾ cup superfine sugar

1 tsp cornstarch

1 oz/25 g semisweet chocolate, grated

filling and topping

6 oz/175 g semisweet chocolate, broken into pieces

2 cups heavy cream, whipped

2 cups fresh raspberries

a little melted chocolate, to decorate

STRAWBERRY ROULADE

Preheat the oven to 425°F/220°C. Line a 14 x 10-inch/35 x 25-cm jelly roll pan with parchment paper.

Place the eggs in a heatproof bowl with the superfine sugar. Place the bowl over a saucepan of hot water and whisk until pale and thick.

Remove the bowl from the pan. Sift in the flour and fold into the egg mixture along with the hot water. Pour the batter into the prepared pan and bake in the preheated oven for 8–10 minutes, until golden and springy to the touch.

Turn out the cake onto a sheet of parchment paper. Peel off the lining paper and roll up the cake tightly along with the parchment paper. Wrap in a clean dish towel and let cool.

For the filling, mix together the mascarpone cheese and the almond extract. Wash, hull, and slice the strawberries. Chill the mascarpone mixture and the strawberries in the refrigerator until ready to use.

Unroll the cake, spread the mascarpone mixture over the surface, and sprinkle with sliced strawberries. Roll up the cake again (without the parchment paper this time) and transfer to a serving plate. Sprinkle with slivered almonds and serve.

SERVES 8

3 eggs

²/₃ cup superfine sugar

scant 1 cup all-purpose flour

1 tbsp hot water

1 tbsp toasted slivered almonds, to decorate

filling

¾ cup low-fat mascarpone cheese

1 tsp almond extract

1½ cups small strawberries

BLACK FOREST ROULADE

SERVES 8–10

sunflower oil, for greasing

6 oz/175 g semisweet chocolate

2–3 tbsp Kirsch or cognac

5 eggs

1 cup superfine sugar

confectioners' sugar, for dusting

filling

1½ cups heavy cream

1 tbsp Kirsch or cognac

12 oz/350 g fresh black cherries,
pitted, or 14 oz/400 g canned
sour cherries, drained and pitted

Preheat the oven to 375°F/190°C. Lightly oil and line a 14 x 10-inch/
35 x 25-cm jelly roll pan with parchment paper.

Break the chocolate into small pieces and place in a heatproof
bowl set over a saucepan of gently simmering water. Add the
Kirsch and heat gently, stirring until the mixture is smooth.
Remove from the pan and set aside.

Place the eggs and superfine sugar in a large heatproof bowl
and set over the pan of gently simmering water. Whisk the eggs
and sugar until very thick and creamy and the whisk leaves a
trail when dragged across the surface. Remove from the heat and
whisk in the cooled chocolate mixture.

Spoon into the prepared jelly roll pan, then tap the pan lightly
on a counter to smooth the top. Bake in the preheated oven for
20 minutes, or until firm to the touch. Remove from the oven and
immediately invert onto a sheet of parchment paper that has
been dusted with confectioners' sugar. Lift off the pan and its
lining paper, then roll up, encasing the new parchment paper in
the roulade. Let stand until cooled.

For the filling, whip the cream until soft peaks form, then stir
in the Kirsch. Unroll the roulade and spread over the cream to
within ¼ inch/5 mm of the edges. Scatter the cherries over the
cream. Carefully roll up the roulade again and place on a serving
platter.

BAKED LEMON CHEESECAKE

Preheat the oven to 350°F/180°C. Lightly grease an 8-inch/
20-cm round springform pan and line the bottom with nonstick
parchment paper.

Melt the butter and stir in the cookie crumbs. Press into the
bottom of the prepared cake pan. Chill until firm.

Meanwhile, finely grate the rind and squeeze the juice from the
lemons. Add the ricotta, yogurt, eggs, cornstarch, and superfine
sugar and whip until a smooth batter is formed.

Carefully pour the batter into the pan. Bake in the preheated
oven for 40–45 minutes, or until just firm and golden brown.

Cool the cheesecake completely in the pan, then run a knife
around the edge to loosen and turn out onto a serving plate.
Decorate with lemon zest and dust with confectioners' sugar.

SERVES 6–8

¼ cup butter, plus extra for
  greasing

3 cups crushed gingersnaps

3 lemons

1⅓ cups ricotta cheese

scant 1 cup Greek-style yogurt or
  strained plain yogurt

4 eggs

1 tbsp cornstarch

½ cup superfine sugar

strips of lemon zest, to decorate

confectioners' sugar, for dusting

BROWNIE CHEESECAKE

Preheat the oven to 350°F/180°C. Lightly grease and flour a 9-inch/23-cm springform round cake pan.

Melt the butter and chocolate in a saucepan over low heat, stirring frequently, until smooth. Remove from the heat and beat in the sugar.

Add the eggs and milk, beating well. Stir in the flour, mixing just until blended. Spoon into the prepared pan, spreading evenly.

Bake in the preheated oven for 25 minutes. Remove from the oven while preparing the topping. Reduce the oven temperature to 325°F/160°C.

For the topping, beat together the cream cheese, sugar, eggs, and vanilla extract until well blended. Stir in the yogurt, then pour into the pan. Bake for an additional 45–55 minutes, or until the center is almost set.

Run a knife around the edge of the cheesecake to loosen from the pan. Let cool before removing from the pan. Chill in the refrigerator for 4 hours or overnight before cutting into slices. Drizzle with the melted chocolate and serve with chocolate-dipped strawberries.

SERVES 12

½ cup unsalted butter, plus extra for greasing

4 oz/115 g semisweet chocolate, broken into pieces

1 cup superfine sugar

2 eggs, beaten

¼ cup milk

1 cup all-purpose flour, plus extra for dusting

chocolate-dipped strawberries, to serve

topping

2¼ cups cream cheese

⅔ cup superfine sugar

3 eggs, beaten

1 tsp vanilla extract

½ cup plain yogurt

melted chocolate, for drizzling

SMALL CAKES & BARS

LOWFAT BLUEBERRY MUFFINS

Preheat the oven to 375°F/190°C. Place 12 muffin paper liners in a muffin pan.

Sift the flour, baking soda, salt, and half of the allspice into a large mixing bowl. Add 6 tablespoons of the superfine sugar and mix together.

In a separate bowl, whisk the egg whites together. Add the margarine, yogurt, and vanilla extract and mix together well, then stir in the blueberries until thoroughly mixed. Add to the flour mixture, then gently stir together until just combined. Do not overstir the batter—it is fine for it to be a little lumpy.

Divide the muffin batter evenly among the paper liners (they should be about two-thirds full). Mix the remaining sugar with the remaining allspice, then sprinkle the mixture over the muffins.

Bake in the preheated oven for 25 minutes, or until risen and golden. Remove the muffins from the oven and serve warm, or place them on a wire rack and let cool.

MAKES 12

generous 1½ cups all-purpose flour

1 tsp baking soda

¼ tsp salt

1 tsp allspice

generous ½ cup superfine sugar

3 egg whites

3 tbsp lowfat margarine

⅔ cup thick lowfat plain yogurt or blueberry-flavored yogurt

1 tsp vanilla extract

¾ cup fresh blueberries

LEMON & POPPY SEED MUFFINS

Preheat the oven to 375°F/190°C. Place 12 muffin paper liners in a muffin pan.

Sift the flour and baking powder into a large bowl and stir in the sugar.

Heat a heavy skillet over medium–high heat and add the poppy seeds. Toast the poppy seeds for about 30 seconds, shaking the skillet to prevent them from burning. Remove from the heat and add to the flour mixture.

Melt the butter, then beat with the egg, milk, lemon rind, and lemon juice. Pour into the dry mixture and stir well to mix evenly to a soft, sticky dough. Add a little more milk if the mixture is too dry.

Spoon the batter into the paper liners, then bake in the preheated oven for 25–30 minutes, or until risen and golden brown. Lift onto a wire rack to cool.

MAKES 12

3 cups all-purpose flour

1 tbsp baking powder

generous ½ cup superfine sugar

2 tbsp poppy seeds

4 tbsp butter

1 extra-large egg, beaten

1 cup milk

finely grated rind and juice of 1 lemon

DOUBLE CHOCOLATE MUFFINS

MAKES 12

scant ½ cup butter, softened

scant ¾ cup superfine sugar

½ cup dark brown sugar

2 eggs

⅔ cup sour cream

5 tbsp milk

2 cups all-purpose flour

1 tsp baking soda

2 tbsp unsweetened cocoa

1 cup semisweet chocolate chips

Preheat the oven to 375°F/190°C. Place 12 muffin paper liners in a muffin pan.

Put the butter, superfine sugar, and brown sugar into a bowl and beat well. Beat in the eggs, sour cream, and milk until thoroughly mixed. Sift the flour, baking soda, and cocoa into a separate bowl and stir into the mixture. Add the chocolate chips and mix well.

Spoon the batter into the paper liners. Bake in the preheated oven for 25–30 minutes. Remove from the oven and let cool for 10 minutes. Turn out onto a wire rack and let cool completely.

FROSTED CUPCAKES

Preheat the oven to 375°F/190°C. Place 16 paper liners in a shallow muffin pan.

Place the butter and sugar in a large bowl and cream together with a wooden spoon or electric mixer until pale and fluffy.

Gradually add the eggs, beating well after each addition. Fold in the flour lightly and evenly using a metal spoon.

Divide the batter among the paper liners and bake in the preheated oven for 15–20 minutes. Cool on a wire rack.

For the frosting, sift the confectioners' sugar into a bowl and stir in just enough of the water to mix to a smooth paste that is thick enough to coat the back of a wooden spoon. Stir in a few drops of food coloring, if using. Spread the frosting over the cupcakes and decorate as desired.

MAKES 16

½ cup butter, softened

generous ½ cup superfine sugar

2 eggs, beaten

1 cup self-rising flour

frosting and decoration

1¾ cups confectioners' sugar

about 2 tbsp warm water

a few drops of edible food coloring (optional)

sugar flowers, sprinkles, candied cherries, and/or chocolate strands, to decorate

CHOCOLATE BUTTERFLY CAKES

Preheat the oven to 350°F/180°C. Place 12 paper liners in a shallow muffin pan.

Place the butter, superfine sugar, flour, eggs, and cocoa in a large bowl and beat with an electric mixer until the mixture is just smooth. Beat in the melted chocolate.

Spoon the batter into the paper liners, filling them three-quarters full. Bake in the preheated oven for 15 minutes, or until springy to the touch. Transfer to a wire rack and let cool.

Meanwhile, make the lemon buttercream. Place the butter in a mixing bowl and beat until fluffy, then gradually beat in the confectioners' sugar. Beat in the lemon rind and gradually add the lemon juice, beating well.

Cut the tops off the cakes using a serrated knife. Cut each cake top in half. Spread or pipe the buttercream over the cut surface of each cake and push the two cut pieces of cake top into the buttercream to form wings. Dust with confectioners' sugar.

MAKES 12

½ cup butter

½ cup superfine sugar

1¼ cups self-rising flour

2 eggs

2 tbsp unsweetened cocoa

1 oz/25 g semisweet chocolate, melted

confectioners' sugar, for dusting

lemon buttercream

6 tbsp butter, softened

1⅓ cups confectioners' sugar, sifted

grated rind of ½ lemon

1 tbsp lemon juice

HONEY & SPICE CUPCAKES

MAKES 22–24

²⁄₃ cup butter

scant ½ cup light brown sugar

scant ½ cup honey

1¾ cups self-rising flour

1 tsp ground allspice

2 eggs, beaten

22–24 whole blanched almonds

Preheat the oven to 350°F/180°C. Place paper liners in two 12-cup shallow muffin pans.

Place the butter, sugar, and honey in a large saucepan and heat gently, stirring, until the butter has melted. Remove the pan from the heat.

Sift together the flour and allspice and stir into the mixture in the pan, then beat in the eggs, mixing to a smooth batter.

Spoon the batter into the paper liners and place a blanched almond on top of each one. Bake in the preheated oven for 20–25 minutes, or until well-risen and golden brown. Transfer to a wire rack to cool.

CARAMEL APPLE CUPCAKES

Preheat the oven to 400°F/200°C. Grease a 12-cup muffin pan (preferably nonstick).

Core and coarsely grate one of the apples. Slice the remaining apple into ¼ inch/5 mm thick wedges and toss in the lemon juice. Sift together the flour, baking powder, and cinnamon, then stir in the sugar and grated apple.

Melt the butter and mix with the milk, apple juice, and egg. Stir the liquid mixture into the dry ingredients, mixing lightly until just combined.

Spoon the batter into the prepared muffin pan. Put two apple slices on top of each cake.

Bake in the preheated oven for 20–25 minutes, or until risen, firm, and golden brown. Run a knife around the edge of each cake to loosen, then turn out onto a wire rack to cool.

For the caramel topping, place all the ingredients in a small saucepan and heat, stirring, until the sugar has dissolved. Increase the heat and boil rapidly for 2 minutes, or until slightly thickened and syrupy. Cool slightly, then drizzle over the cakes and let set.

MAKES 12

2 apples

1 tbsp lemon juice

2¼ cups all-purpose flour

2 tsp baking powder

1½ tsp ground cinnamon

generous ¼ cup light brown sugar

4 tbsp butter, plus extra for greasing

scant ½ cup milk

scant ½ cup apple juice

1 egg, beaten

caramel topping

2 tbsp light cream

3 tbsp light brown sugar

1 tbsp butter

CHOCOLATE FONDUE CUPCAKES

MAKES 8

4 tbsp soft margarine
¼ cup superfine sugar
1 large egg
½ cup self-rising flour
1 tbsp unsweetened cocoa
2 oz/55 g semisweet chocolate
confectioners' sugar, for dusting

Preheat the oven to 375°F/190°C. Put 8 paper liners into a shallow muffin pan.

Put the margarine, superfine sugar, egg, flour, and cocoa in a large bowl and, using a handheld electric mixer, beat together until just smooth.

Spoon half of the batter into the paper liners. Using a teaspoon, make an indentation in the center of each cake. Break the chocolate evenly into eight squares and place a piece in each indentation, then spoon the remaining cake batter on top.

Bake the cupcakes in the preheated oven for 20 minutes, or until well risen and springy to the touch. Let the cupcakes cool for 2–3 minutes before serving warm, dusted with confectioners' sugar.

DOUBLE CHOCOLATE BROWNIES

MAKES 9

½ cup butter, plus extra
   for greasing

4 oz/115 g semisweet chocolate,
   broken into pieces

1⅓ cups superfine sugar

pinch of salt

1 tsp vanilla extract

2 eggs

1 cup all-purpose flour

2 tbsp unsweetened cocoa

½ cup white chocolate chips

fudge sauce

4 tbsp butter

generous 1 cup superfine sugar

⅔ cup milk

generous 1 cup heavy cream

⅔ cup dark corn syrup

7 oz/200 g semisweet chocolate,
   broken into pieces

Preheat the oven to 350°F/180°C. Grease a 7-inch/18-cm square cake pan and line the bottom with parchment paper.

Place the butter and chocolate in a small heatproof bowl set over a saucepan of gently simmering water until melted. Stir until smooth. Let cool slightly. Stir in the sugar, salt, and vanilla extract. Add the eggs, one at a time, stirring well, until blended.

Sift the flour and cocoa into the cake batter and beat until smooth. Stir in the chocolate chips, then pour the batter into the prepared pan. Bake in the preheated oven for 35–40 minutes, or until the top is evenly colored and a toothpick inserted into the center comes out almost clean. Let cool slightly while you prepare the sauce.

To make the sauce, place the butter, sugar, milk, cream, and corn syrup in a small saucepan and heat gently until the sugar has dissolved. Bring to a boil and stir for 10 minutes, or until the mixture is caramel-colored. Remove from the heat and add the chocolate. Stir until smooth. Cut the brownies into squares and serve immediately with the sauce.

CAPPUCCINO BROWNIES

Grease an 11 x 7-inch/28 x 18-cm shallow cake pan and line the bottom with parchment paper.

Sift the flour, baking powder, and cocoa into a bowl and add the butter, superfine sugar, eggs, and coffee. Beat well, by hand or with an electric whisk, until smooth, then spoon into the prepared pan and smooth the top.

Bake in the preheated oven for 35–40 minutes, or until risen and firm. Let cool in the pan for 10 minutes, then turn out onto a wire rack and peel off the lining paper. Let cool completely.

To make the frosting, place the chocolate, butter, and milk in a bowl set over a saucepan of gently simmering water and stir until the chocolate has melted.

Remove the bowl from the pan and sift in the confectioners' sugar. Beat until smooth, then spread over the cake. Dust the top of the cake with cocoa, then cut into squares.

MAKES 15

generous 1½ cups self-rising flour

1 tsp baking powder

1 tsp unsweetened cocoa, plus extra for dusting

1 cup butter, softened, plus extra for greasing

generous 1 cup superfine sugar

4 eggs, beaten

3 tbsp instant coffee powder, dissolved in 2 tbsp hot water

white chocolate frosting

4 oz/115 g white chocolate, broken into pieces

4 tbsp butter, softened

3 tbsp milk

1¾ cups confectioners' sugar

COCONUT BARS

Preheat the oven to 350°F/180°C. Grease a 9-inch/23-cm square cake pan and line the bottom with nonstick parchment paper.

Cream together the butter and superfine sugar until pale and fluffy, then gradually beat in the eggs. Stir in the orange rind, orange juice, and sour cream. Fold in the flour and dry unsweetened coconut evenly using a metal spoon.

Spoon the batter into the prepared cake pan and level the surface. Bake in the preheated oven for 35–40 minutes, or until risen and firm to the touch.

Let cool for 10 minutes in the pan, then turn out and finish cooling on a wire rack.

For the frosting, lightly beat the egg white, just enough to break it up, and stir in the confectioners' sugar and dry unsweetened coconut, adding enough orange juice to mix to a thick paste. Spread over the top of the cake, sprinkle with long shred coconut, then let set before slicing into bars.

MAKES 10

generous ½ cup butter, plus extra
   for greasing
generous 1 cup superfine sugar
2 eggs, beaten
finely grated rind of 1 orange
3 tbsp orange juice
⅔ cup sour cream
1¼ cups self-rising flour
1 cup dry unsweetened coconut
toasted long shred coconut,
   to decorate

frosting
1 egg white
1¾ cups confectioners' sugar
1 cup dry unsweetened coconut
about 1 tbsp orange juice

ALMOND & RASPBERRY BARS

MAKES 12

dough

1½ cups all-purpose flour

generous ½ cup butter

2 tbsp superfine sugar

1 egg yolk

about 1 tbsp cold water

filling

½ cup butter

generous ½ cup superfine sugar

1 cup ground almonds

3 eggs, beaten

½ tsp almond extract

4 tbsp raspberry jam

2 tbsp slivered almonds

For the dough, sift the flour into a bowl and rub in the butter with your fingertips until the mixture resembles fine breadcrumbs. Stir in the sugar, then combine the egg yolk and water and stir in to make a firm dough, adding a little more water if necessary. Wrap in plastic wrap and chill in the refrigerator for about 15 minutes, until firm enough to roll out.

Preheat the oven to 400°F/200°C. Roll out the dough and use to line a 9-inch/23-cm square tart pan or shallow cake pan. Prick the bottom and chill for 15 minutes.

For the filling, cream the butter and sugar together until pale and fluffy, then beat in the ground almonds, eggs, and almond extract.

Spread the jam over the bottom of the pastry shell, then top with the almond filling, spreading it evenly. Sprinkle with the slivered almonds.

Bake in the preheated oven for 10 minutes, then reduce the temperature to 350°F/180°C and bake for an additional 25–30 minutes, or until the filling is golden brown and firm to the touch. Cool in the pan, then cut into bars.

LEMON DRIZZLE BARS

Preheat the oven to 350°F/180°C. Grease a 7-inch/18-cm square cake pan and line with nonstick parchment paper.

Place the eggs, superfine sugar, and margarine in a bowl and beat hard until smooth and fluffy. Stir in the lemon rind, then fold in the flour lightly and evenly. Stir in the milk, mixing evenly, then spoon into the prepared cake pan, smoothing level.

Bake in the preheated oven for 45–50 minutes, or until golden brown and firm to the touch. Remove from the oven and place the pan on a wire rack.

To make the syrup, place the confectioners' sugar and lemon juice in a small saucepan and heat gently, stirring until the sugar dissolves. Do not boil.

Prick the warm cake all over with a skewer and spoon the hot syrup evenly over the top.

Let cool completely in the pan, then turn out the cake, cut into 12 pieces, and dust with a little confectioners' sugar before serving.

MAKES 12

2 eggs

generous ¾ cup superfine sugar

⅔ cup soft margarine, plus extra for greasing

finely grated rind of 1 lemon

1½ cups self-rising flour

½ cup milk

confectioners' sugar, for dusting

syrup

1¼ cups confectioners' sugar

¼ cup fresh lemon juice

CINNAMON SQUARES

Preheat the oven to 350°F/180°C. Grease a 9-inch/23-cm square cake pan and line the bottom with parchment paper.

In a large mixing bowl, cream together the butter and superfine sugar until light and fluffy. Gradually add the eggs, beating thoroughly after each addition.

Sift the flour, baking soda, and cinnamon together into the creamed mixture and fold in evenly using a metal spoon. Spoon in the sour cream and sunflower seeds and mix gently until well combined.

Spoon the batter into the prepared cake pan and smooth the surface.

Bake in the preheated oven for about 45 minutes, until firm to the touch. Loosen the edges with a knife, then turn out onto a wire rack to cool completely. Slice into squares before serving.

MAKES 16

1 cup butter, softened, plus extra for greasing

1¼ cups superfine sugar

3 eggs, lightly beaten

1¾ cups self-rising flour

½ tsp baking soda

1 tbsp ground cinnamon

⅔ cup sour cream

½ cup sunflower seeds

COCONUT-COVERED SPONGE CAKES

MAKES 16

6 eggs

¾ cup superfine sugar

1½ cups all-purpose flour

¼ cup unsalted butter, melted, plus extra for greasing

3 cups dry unsweetened coconut

frosting

4½ cups confectioners' sugar

⅓ cup unsweetened cocoa

⅓ cup boiling water

5 tbsp unsalted butter, melted

Preheat the oven to 350°F/180°C. Grease an 8-inch/20-cm square cake pan and line the bottom with parchment paper.

Place the eggs and superfine sugar in a large bowl set over a saucepan of gently simmering water and whisk until pale and thick enough to leave a trail when the whisk is lifted.

Remove from the heat, sift in the flour, and fold in evenly. Fold in the melted butter. Pour into the prepared pan and bake in the preheated oven for 35–40 minutes, or until risen, golden, and springy to the touch.

Cool in the pan for 2–3 minutes, then turn out onto a wire rack to finish cooling. When cold, cut the cake into 16 squares.

For the frosting, sift together the confectioners' sugar and cocoa into a bowl and stir in the water and butter, mixing until smooth. Spread out the dry unsweetened coconut on a large plate. Dip each piece of sponge cake into the frosting, using two spatulas to turn and coat evenly. Place in the dry unsweetened coconut and turn to coat evenly. Place on a sheet of parchment paper and let set.

NUTTY OAT BARS

SMALL CAKES & BARS

Preheat the oven to 350°F/180°C. Grease a 9-inch/23-cm square cake pan.

Place the rolled oats, hazelnuts, and flour in a large mixing bowl and stir together.

Place the butter, corn syrup, and sugar in a saucepan over low heat and stir until melted. Pour onto the dry ingredients and mix well. Spoon into the prepared cake pan and smooth the surface with the back of a spoon.

Bake in the preheated oven for 20–25 minutes, or until golden and firm to the touch. Mark into 16 pieces and let cool in the pan. When completely cooled, cut through with a sharp knife and remove from the pan.

MAKES 16

scant 2¾ cups rolled oats

¾ cup chopped hazelnuts

6 tbsp all-purpose flour

½ cup butter, plus extra
for greasing

2 tbsp dark corn syrup

scant ½ cup light brown sugar

CHOCOLATE PEANUT BUTTER SQUARES

Preheat the oven to 350°F/180°C.

Finely chop the chocolate. Sift the flour and baking powder into a large bowl. Add the butter to the flour mixture and rub in using your fingertips until the mixture resembles breadcrumbs. Stir in the sugar, rolled oats, and chopped nuts.

Put a quarter of the mixture into a bowl and stir in the chocolate. Set aside.

Stir the egg into the remaining mixture, then press into the bottom of a 12 x 8-inch/30 x 20-cm cake pan. Bake in the preheated oven for 15 minutes.

Meanwhile, mix the condensed milk and peanut butter together. Pour into the cake pan and spread evenly, then sprinkle the reserved chocolate mixture on top and press down lightly.

Return to the oven and bake for an additional 20 minutes, until golden brown. Let cool in the pan, then cut into squares.

MAKES 25

10½ oz/300 g milk chocolate

2½ cups all-purpose flour

1 tsp baking powder

1 cup butter

1¾ cups light brown sugar

2 cups rolled oats

½ cup chopped mixed nuts

1 egg, beaten

14 oz/400 g canned sweetened condensed milk

⅓ cup crunchy peanut butter

CHOCOLATE CARAMEL SHORTBREAD

MAKES 12

½ cup butter, plus extra
  for greasing

generous 1 cup all-purpose flour

generous ¼ cup superfine sugar

filling and topping

¾ cup butter

generous ½ cup superfine sugar

3 tbsp dark corn syrup

14 oz/400 g canned sweetened
  condensed milk

7 oz/200 g semisweet chocolate,
  broken into pieces

Preheat the oven to 350°F/180°C. Grease a 9-inch/23-cm shallow square cake pan and line the bottom with parchment paper.

Place the butter, flour, and sugar in a food processor and process until it starts to bind together. Press into the prepared pan and level the top. Bake in the preheated oven for 20–25 minutes, or until golden.

Meanwhile, make the caramel. Place the butter, sugar, corn syrup, and condensed milk in a heavy-bottom saucepan. Heat gently until the sugar has dissolved. Bring to a boil, then reduce the heat and let simmer for 6–8 minutes, stirring, until very thick. Pour over the shortbread and let chill in the refrigerator for 2 hours, or until firm.

Place the chocolate in a heatproof bowl set over a saucepan of gently simmering water and stir until melted. Let cool slightly, then spread over the caramel. Let chill in the refrigerator for 2 hours, or until set. Cut the shortbread into 12 pieces using a sharp knife and serve.

CHOCOLATE PEPPERMINT BARS

Preheat the oven to 350°F/180°C. Grease a 12 x 8-inch/30 x 20-cm jelly roll pan and line with parchment paper.

Beat the butter and sugar together until pale and fluffy. Stir in the flour until the mixture binds together.

Knead the mixture to form a smooth dough, then press into the prepared pan. Prick the surface all over with a fork. Bake in the preheated oven for 10–15 minutes, or until lightly browned and just firm to the touch. Remove from the oven and let cool in the pan.

Sift the confectioners' sugar into a bowl. Gradually add the water, then add the peppermint extract and the food coloring, if using. Spread the frosting over the base, then let set.

Melt the chocolate in a heatproof bowl set over a saucepan of gently simmering water, then remove from the heat and spread over the frosting. Let set, then cut into slices.

MAKES 16

½ cup unsalted butter, plus extra for greasing

½ cup superfine sugar

generous 1⅓ cups all-purpose flour

2½ cups confectioners' sugar

2–4 tbsp warm water

1 tsp peppermint extract

a few drops of green edible food coloring (optional)

6 oz/175 g semisweet chocolate, broken into pieces

STRAWBERRY SHORTCAKES

Preheat the oven to 350°F/180°C and lightly grease a large baking sheet.

Sift the flour, baking powder, and superfine sugar into a bowl. Rub in the butter with your fingertips until the mixture resembles breadcrumbs. Beat the egg with 2 tablespoons of the milk and stir into the dry ingredients with a fork to form a soft, but not sticky, dough, adding more milk if necessary.

Turn out the dough onto a lightly floured counter and roll out to a thickness of about ¾ inch/2 cm. Stamp out rounds using a 2¾-inch/7-cm cookie cutter. Press the trimmings together lightly and stamp out more rounds.

Place the rounds on the prepared baking sheet and brush the tops lightly with milk. Bake in the preheated oven for 12–15 minutes, until firm and golden brown. Lift onto a wire rack to cool.

For the filling, stir the vanilla into the mascarpone cheese with 2 tablespoons of the confectioners' sugar. Reserve a few whole strawberries for decoration, then hull and slice the remainder. Sprinkle with the remaining 1 tablespoon of confectioners' sugar.

Split the shortcakes in half horizontally. Spoon half the mascarpone mixture onto the bottom halves and top with sliced strawberries. Spoon over the remaining mascarpone mixture and replace the shortcake tops. To serve, dust with confectioners' sugar and top with the reserved whole strawberries.

SERVES 6

2 cups self-rising flour, plus extra for dusting

½ tsp baking powder

½ cup superfine sugar

6 tbsp unsalted butter, plus extra for greasing

1 egg, beaten

2–3 tbsp milk, plus extra for brushing

filling

1 tsp vanilla extract

generous 1 cup mascarpone cheese

3 tbsp confectioners' sugar, plus extra for dusting

3½ cups strawberries

SCONES

MAKES 10–12

3½ cups all-purpose flour, plus extra for dusting

½ tsp salt

2 tsp baking powder

4 tbsp butter

2 tbsp superfine sugar

1 cup milk, plus extra for glazing

strawberry preserves and whipped heavy cream, to serve

Preheat the oven to 425°F/220°C.

Sift the flour, salt, and baking powder into a bowl. Rub in the butter using your fingertips until the mixture resembles breadcrumbs. Stir in the sugar.

Make a well in the center and pour in the milk. Stir in using a spatula to form a soft dough.

Turn out the dough onto a floured surface and lightly flatten until it is of an even thickness, about ½ inch/1 cm. Don't be heavy-handed; scones need a light touch.

Cut out the scones using a 2½-inch/6-cm cookie cutter and place on a cookie sheet.

Brush with a little milk and bake in the preheated oven for 10–12 minutes, until golden and well risen. Cool on a wire rack and serve freshly baked with strawberry preserves and whipped heavy cream.

ROCK CAKES

Preheat the oven to 400°F/200°C. Lightly grease two cookie sheets.

Sift the flour and baking powder into a large bowl and rub in the butter using your fingertips until it resembles fine breadcrumbs. Stir in the light brown sugar, mixed dried fruit, and lemon rind.

Beat the egg lightly with a tablespoon of the milk and stir into the flour mixture, adding a little more milk if necessary, until it starts to bind together to form a moist but firm dough.

Spoon small heaps of the mixture on the prepared cookie sheets. Sprinkle with the raw brown sugar.

Bake in the preheated oven for 15–20 minutes, or until golden brown and firm. Use a metal spatula to transfer the cakes onto a wire rack to cool.

MAKES 8–10

- 2 cups all-purpose flour
- 2 tsp baking powder
- ½ cup butter, plus extra for greasing
- ⅓ cup light brown sugar
- ⅓ cup mixed dried fruit
- finely grated rind of 1 lemon
- 1 egg
- 1–2 tbsp milk
- 2 tsp raw brown sugar

CHOCOLATE MERINGUES

Preheat the oven to 275°F/140°C. Line two cookie sheets with parchment paper.

Whisk the egg whites until soft peaks form, then gradually whisk in half of the superfine sugar. Continue whisking until the mixture is very stiff and glossy.

Carefully fold in the remaining sugar, the cornstarch, and grated chocolate with a metal spoon or spatula.

Spoon the mixture into a pastry bag fitted with a large star or plain tip. Pipe 16 large rosettes or mounds onto the prepared cookie sheets.

Bake in the preheated oven for about 1 hour, changing the position of the cookie sheets after 30 minutes. Without opening the oven door, turn off the oven and let the meringues cool in the oven. Once cold, carefully peel off the parchment paper.

To make the filling, melt the chocolate in a heatproof bowl set over a saucepan of gently simmering water and carefully spread it over the bottom of the meringues. Stand them upside down on a wire rack until the chocolate has set. Whip the cream, confectioners' sugar, and cognac, if using, until the cream holds its shape, then use to sandwich the chocolate-coated meringues together in pairs.

MAKES 8

4 egg whites

1 cup superfine sugar

1 tsp cornstarch

1½ oz/40 g semisweet chocolate, grated

filling

3½ oz/100 g semisweet chocolate

⅔ cup heavy cream

1 tbsp confectioners' sugar

1 tbsp cognac (optional)

ALMOND MACAROONS

MAKES 12–14

1 egg white

¾ cup ground almonds

scant ½ cup superfine sugar, plus extra for rolling

½ tsp almond extract

6–7 blanched almonds, split in half

Preheat the oven to 350°F/180°C. Line two baking sheets with parchment paper.

Beat the egg white with a fork until frothy, then stir in the ground almonds, sugar, and almond extract, mixing to form a sticky dough.

Using lightly sugared hands, roll the dough into small balls and place on the prepared baking sheets. Press an almond half into the center of each.

Bake in the preheated oven for 15–20 minutes, or until pale golden. Lift onto a wire rack to cool.

MADELEINES

Preheat the oven to 375°F/190°C. Lightly grease 30 cups in 2–3 standard-size madeleine pans.

Place the eggs, egg yolk, vanilla extract, and sugar in a large bowl and whisk with a handheld electric mixer until very pale and thick.

Sift in the flour and baking powder and fold in lightly and evenly using a metal spoon. Fold in the melted butter evenly.

Spoon the batter into the prepared pans, filling to about three-quarters full. Bake in the preheated oven for 8–10 minutes, until risen and golden.

Remove the cakes carefully from the pans and cool on a wire rack. They are best served the day they are made.

MAKES 30

3 eggs

1 egg yolk

1 tsp vanilla extract

¾ cup superfine sugar

1¼ cups all-purpose flour

1 tsp baking powder

⅔ cup unsalted butter, melted and cooled, plus extra for greasing

PIES & PASTRIES

APPLE PIE

To make the pie dough, sift the flour and salt into a large bowl. Add the butter and lard and rub in using your fingertips until the mixture resembles fine breadcrumbs. Add the water and gather the mixture together into a dough. Wrap the dough and let chill in the refrigerator for 30 minutes.

Preheat the oven to 425°F/220°C. Roll out almost two thirds of the pie dough thinly and use to line a deep 9-inch/23-cm pie plate.

Mix the apples with the sugar and spice and pack into the pastry shell; the filling can come up above the rim. Add the water if needed, particularly if the apples are a dry variety.

Roll out the remaining pie dough to form a lid. Dampen the edges of the pie rim with water and position the lid, pressing the edges firmly together. Trim and crimp the edges.

Use the trimmings to cut out leaves or other shapes to decorate the top of the pie. Dampen and attach. Glaze the top of the pie with beaten egg or milk, make one or two slits in the top, and place the pie on a baking sheet.

Bake in the preheated oven for 20 minutes, then reduce the temperature to 350°F/180°C and bake for an additional 30 minutes, or until the pastry is a light golden brown. Serve hot or cold, sprinkled with sugar.

SERVES 6–8

pie dough

2 cups all-purpose flour

pinch of salt

6 tbsp butter or margarine, cut into small pieces

6 tbsp lard or vegetable shortening, cut into small pieces

about 6 tbsp cold water

beaten egg or milk, for glazing

filling

1 lb 10 oz–2 lb 4 oz/750 g–1 kg baking apples, peeled, cored, and sliced

scant 2/3 cup light brown sugar or superfine sugar, plus extra for sprinkling

1/2–1 tsp ground cinnamon, allspice, or ground ginger

1–2 tbsp water (optional)

LATTICED CHERRY PIE

To make the pie dough, sift the flour and baking powder into a large bowl. Stir in the allspice, salt, and sugar. Rub in the butter with your fingertips until the mixture resembles fine breadcrumbs. Add the beaten egg and mix to a firm dough. Cut the dough in half and roll each half into a ball. Wrap in plastic wrap and chill in the refrigerator for 30 minutes.

Preheat the oven to 425°F/220°C. Grease a 9-inch/23-cm round tart pan. Roll out the pie dough into two 12-inch/30-cm rounds. Use one to line the tart pan, trimming the edge to leave an overhang of ½ inch/1 cm.

To make the filling, put half of the cherries and the sugar in a large saucepan. Bring to a simmer over low heat, stirring, for 5 minutes, or until the sugar has dissolved. Stir in the almond extract, brandy, and allspice. In a separate bowl, mix the cornstarch and water to form a paste. Remove the saucepan from the heat, stir in the cornstarch paste, then return to the heat and stir continuously until the mixture boils and thickens. Let cool a little. Stir in the remaining cherries, pour into the pastry shell, then dot with the butter.

Cut the remaining dough round into long strips about ½ inch/ 1 cm wide. Lay five strips evenly across the top of the filling in the same direction. Now lay six strips crosswise over the strips, folding back every other strip each time you add another crosswise strip, to form a lattice. Trim off the ends and seal the edges with water. Use your fingers to crimp around the rim, then brush the top with beaten egg to glaze. Cover with foil, then bake in the preheated oven for 30 minutes. Discard the foil, then bake for an additional 15 minutes, or until golden.

SERVES 8

pie dough
1 cup all-purpose flour, plus extra for dusting

¼ tsp baking powder

½ tsp allspice

½ tsp salt

¼ cup superfine sugar

4 tbsp cold unsalted butter, diced, plus extra for greasing

1 egg, beaten, plus extra for glazing

filling
2 lb/900 g pitted fresh cherries or drained canned cherries

½ cup superfine sugar

½ tsp almond extract

2 tsp cherry brandy

¼ tsp allspice

2 tbsp cornstarch

2 tbsp water

2 tbsp unsalted butter, diced

ONE ROLL
FRUIT PIE

SERVES 8

1⅛ cups all-purpose flour, plus
   extra for dusting

scant ½ cup butter, cut into small
   pieces, plus extra for greasing

1 tbsp water

1 egg, separated

crushed sugar cubes,
   for sprinkling

filling

1 lb 5 oz/600 g prepared fruit,
   such as rhubarb, gooseberries,
   or plums

generous ⅓ cup light brown sugar

1 tbsp ground ginger

Place the flour in a large bowl, add the butter, and rub it in with your fingertips until the mixture resembles breadcrumbs. Add the water and mix together to form a soft dough. Cover and let chill in the refrigerator for 30 minutes.

Preheat the oven to 400°F/200°C. Grease a large cookie sheet.

Roll out the dough on a lightly floured counter to a 14-inch/35-cm round. Transfer the round to the prepared cookie sheet and brush with the egg yolk.

To make the filling, mix the fruit with the sugar and ground ginger and pile it into the center of the pie dough. Turn in the edges of the dough all the way around. Brush the surface of the dough with the egg white and sprinkle with the crushed sugar cubes.

Bake in the preheated oven for 35 minutes, or until golden brown. Transfer to a serving plate and serve warm.

TARTE TATIN

Preheat the oven to 425°F/220°C.

For the pie dough, sift the flour into a bowl. Rub in the butter with your fingertips until the mixture resembles fine breadcrumbs. Stir in the sugar, then add the egg yolks and water, mixing lightly until it just binds together. Wrap in plastic wrap and chill in the refrigerator for 10–15 minutes.

Meanwhile, for the filling, place the butter and sugar in a heavy saucepan with the water. Heat gently until the butter has melted, then bring to a boil. Boil rapidly, stirring occasionally, until the mixture turns to a rich, golden caramel color. Pour quickly into a 9-inch/23-cm round cake pan (this needs to be 2 inches/5 cm deep with a rigid bottom), tilting to cover the bottom.

Peel, core, and thickly slice the apples, toss with the lemon juice, and arrange over the caramel in the pan.

Roll out the dough on a lightly floured counter to a round large enough to fit the cake pan. Lift the dough onto the apples and tuck in the edges.

Place on a baking sheet and bake in the preheated oven for about 40 minutes, or until the pastry is golden. Let stand for 10 minutes, then carefully invert onto a serving plate. Serve warm.

SERVES 6

pie dough

1½ cups all-purpose flour, plus extra for dusting

scant ½ cup cold unsalted butter

3 tbsp superfine sugar

2 egg yolks

2–3 tbsp cold water

filling

⅓ cup unsalted butter

scant ¾ cup superfine sugar

1 tbsp water

6–7 apples

2 tbsp lemon juice

PLUM CRUMBLE TART

Preheat the oven to 350°F/180°C and preheat a cookie sheet.

Sift the flour, cornstarch, and baking powder into a large bowl and rub in the butter using your fingertips until it resembles fine breadcrumbs. Stir in the hazelnuts and sugar with just enough milk to bind together.

Remove about a quarter of the mixture, cover, and place in the refrigerator. Gently knead the remainder together and press into the bottom and sides of an 8-inch/20-cm loose-bottom round tart pan.

For the filling, halve and pit the plums, cut into quarters, and toss with the cornstarch, sugar, and orange rind. Arrange the plums over the dough.

Remove the reserved dough from the refrigerator and, using your fingertips, crumble it over the plums.

Place the tart on the cookie sheet and bake in the preheated oven for 40–45 minutes, until lightly browned and bubbling. Serve warm or cold.

SERVES 8–10

dough
1½ cups all-purpose flour

1 tbsp cornstarch

½ tsp baking powder

7 tbsp butter

⅓ cup finely chopped hazelnuts

scant ¼ cup superfine sugar

2–3 tbsp milk

filling
14 oz/400 g ripe red plums

1 tbsp cornstarch

3 tbsp superfine sugar

finely grated rind of 1 small orange

PEAR TART WITH CHOCOLATE SAUCE

SERVES 6

¾ cup all-purpose flour

¼ cup ground almonds

5 tbsp block margarine, plus extra
  for greasing

about 3 tbsp water

filling

4 tbsp butter

4 tbsp superfine sugar

2 eggs, beaten

1 cup ground almonds

2 tbsp unsweetened cocoa

a few drops of almond extract

14 oz/400 g canned pear halves in
  natural juice, drained

chocolate sauce

4 tbsp superfine sugar

3 tbsp dark corn syrup

generous ⅓ cup water

6 oz/175 g semisweet chocolate,
  broken into pieces

2 tbsp butter

Preheat the oven to 400°F/200°C. Lightly grease an 8-inch/20-cm round tart pan.

Sift the flour into a mixing bowl and stir in the ground almonds. Rub in the margarine with your fingertips until the mixture resembles breadcrumbs. Add enough of the water to mix to a soft dough. Cover, chill in the freezer for 10 minutes, then roll out and use to line the prepared pan. Prick the bottom with a fork and chill again.

To make the filling, beat the butter and sugar until light and fluffy. Beat in the eggs, then fold in the ground almonds, cocoa, and almond extract. Spread the chocolate mixture in the pastry shell. Thinly slice the pears widthwise, flatten slightly, then arrange the slices on top of the chocolate mixture, pressing down lightly. Bake in the preheated oven for 30 minutes, or until the filling has risen. Cool slightly and transfer to a serving dish, if you want.

To make the chocolate sauce, place the sugar, corn syrup, and water in a saucepan and heat gently, stirring until the sugar dissolves. Boil gently for 1 minute. Remove from the heat, add the chocolate and butter, and stir until melted. Serve with the tart.

LEMON MERINGUE PIE

To make the pie dough, sift the flour into a bowl. Rub in the butter using your fingertips until the mixture resembles fine breadcrumbs. Mix in the remaining ingredients. Knead briefly on a lightly floured counter. Let rest for 30 minutes.

Preheat the oven to 350°F/180°C. Grease an 8-inch/20-cm round tart pan. Roll out the pie dough to a thickness of ¼ inch/ 5 mm and use it to line the bottom and sides of the prepared pan. Prick all over with a fork, line with parchment paper, and fill with dried beans. Bake in the preheated oven for 15 minutes. Remove from the oven and take out the parchment paper and dried beans. Reduce the temperature to 300°F/150°C.

To make the filling, mix the cornstarch with a little of the water. Place the remaining water in a saucepan. Stir in the lemon juice and rind and the cornstarch paste. Bring to a boil, stirring. Cook for 2 minutes. Let cool a little. Stir in 5 tablespoons of the superfine sugar and the egg yolks, then pour into the pastry shell.

Whip the egg whites in a clean, greasefree bowl until stiff. Whip in the remaining superfine sugar and spread over the pie. Bake for an additional 40 minutes. Remove from the oven, let cool, and serve.

SERVES 6–8

pie dough
generous 1 cup all-purpose flour, plus extra for dusting

6 tbsp butter, cut into small pieces, plus extra for greasing

¼ cup confectioners' sugar, sifted

finely grated rind of ½ lemon

½ egg yolk, beaten

1½ tbsp milk

filling
3 tbsp cornstarch

1¼ cups water

juice and grated rind of 2 lemons

generous ¾ cup superfine sugar

2 eggs, separated

KEY LIME PIE

Preheat the oven to 325°F/160°C. Lightly grease a 9-inch/ 23-cm round tart pan, about 1½ inches/4 cm deep.

To make the crumb crust, place the crackers, sugar, and cinnamon in a food processor and process until fine crumbs form—do not overprocess to a powder. Add the melted butter and process again until moistened.

Tip the crumb mixture into the prepared tart pan and press over the bottom and sides. Place the tart pan on a baking sheet and bake in the preheated oven for 5 minutes.

Meanwhile, beat the condensed milk, lime juice, lime rind, and egg yolks together in a bowl until well blended.

Remove the tart pan from the oven, pour in the filling, and spread out to the edges. Return to the oven for an additional 15 minutes, or until the filling is set around the edges but still wobbly in the center.

Let cool completely on a wire rack, then cover and let chill for at least 2 hours. Serve spread thickly with whipped cream.

SERVES 8

crumb crust
6 oz/175 g graham crackers or gingersnaps

2 tbsp superfine sugar

½ tsp ground cinnamon

5 tbsp butter, melted, plus extra for greasing

filling
1¾ cups canned sweetened condensed milk

½ cup freshly squeezed lime juice

finely grated rind of 3 limes

4 egg yolks

whipped cream, to serve

SWEET PUMPKIN PIE

SERVES 6

4 lb/1.8 kg sweet pumpkin

1 cup all-purpose flour, plus extra for dusting

¼ tsp baking powder

1½ tsp ground cinnamon

¾ tsp ground nutmeg

¾ tsp ground cloves

1 tsp salt

½ cup superfine sugar

4 tbsp cold unsalted butter, diced, plus extra for greasing

3 eggs

1¾ cups canned sweetened condensed milk

½ tsp vanilla extract

1 tbsp raw brown sugar

streusel topping

2 tbsp all-purpose flour

4 tbsp raw brown sugar

1 tsp ground cinnamon

2 tbsp cold unsalted butter, cut into small pieces

generous ⅔ cup chopped pecans

generous ⅔ cup chopped walnuts

Preheat the oven to 375°F/190°C. Halve the pumpkin, then remove and discard the stem, seeds, and stringy insides. Put the pumpkin halves, face down, in a shallow roasting pan and cover with foil. Bake in the preheated oven for 1½ hours, then let cool. Scoop out the flesh and puree in a food processor. Drain off any excess liquid. Cover with plastic wrap and chill until ready to use.

Grease a 9-inch/23-cm round tart pan. To make the pie dough, sift the flour and baking powder into a large bowl. Stir in ½ teaspoon of the cinnamon, ¼ teaspoon of the nutmeg, ¼ teaspoon of the cloves, ½ teaspoon of the salt, and all the superfine sugar. Rub in the butter with your fingertips until the mixture resembles fine breadcrumbs, then make a well in the center. Lightly beat one of the eggs and pour it into the well. Mix together with a wooden spoon, then use your hands to shape the dough into a ball. Place the dough on a lightly floured counter and roll out to a round large enough to line the tart pan. Use it to line the pan, then trim the edges. Cover with plastic wrap and chill in the refrigerator for 30 minutes.

Preheat the oven to 425°F/220°C. To make the filling, put the pumpkin puree in a large bowl, then stir in the condensed milk and the remaining eggs. Add the remaining spices and salt, then stir in the vanilla extract and brown sugar. Pour into the pastry shell and bake in the preheated oven for 15 minutes.

Meanwhile, make the topping. Combine the flour, brown sugar, and cinnamon in a bowl, rub in the butter, then stir in the nuts. Remove the pie from the oven and reduce the heat to 350°F/180°C. Sprinkle over the pie, then bake for an additional 35 minutes.

SWEET POTATO PIE

To make the pie dough, sift the flour, salt, and superfine sugar into a bowl. Add the butter and shortening to the bowl and rub in with your fingertips until the mixture resembles fine breadcrumbs. Sprinkle over 2 tablespoons of the water and mix with a fork to make a soft dough. If the dough is too dry, sprinkle in the extra ½ tablespoon of water. Wrap the dough in plastic wrap and chill in the refrigerator for at least 1 hour.

Meanwhile, bring a large saucepan of water to a boil over high heat. Add the sweet potatoes and cook for 15 minutes. Drain, then cool under cold running water. When cool, cut each into eight wedges. Place the potatoes in a bowl and beat in the eggs and brown sugar until very smooth. Beat in the remaining ingredients, then set aside until required.

Preheat the oven to 425°F/220°C. Roll out the pie dough on a lightly floured counter into a thin 11-inch/28-cm round and use to line a 9-inch/23-cm round tart pan, about 1½ inches/4 cm deep. Trim off the excess dough and press a floured fork around the edge. Prick the bottom of the pastry shell all over with the fork. Line with parchment paper and fill with dried beans. Bake in the preheated oven for 12 minutes, until lightly golden. Remove from the oven and take out the paper and beans.

Pour the filling into the pastry shell and return to the oven for an additional 10 minutes. Reduce the oven temperature to 325°F/160°C and bake for an additional 35 minutes, or until a knife inserted into the center comes out clean. Let cool on a wire rack. Serve warm or at room temperature.

SERVES 8

pie dough

1¼ cups all-purpose flour, plus extra for dusting

½ tsp salt

¼ tsp superfine sugar

1½ tbsp butter, diced

3 tbsp shortening, diced

2–2½ tbsp cold water

filling

1 lb 2 oz/500 g orange-fleshed sweet potatoes, peeled

3 extra-large eggs, beaten

½ cup firmly packed light brown sugar

1½ cups canned condensed milk

3 tbsp butter, melted

2 tsp vanilla extract

1 tsp ground cinnamon

1 tsp ground nutmeg

½ tsp salt

PECAN PIE

For the pie dough, place the flour in a bowl and rub in the butter using your fingertips until it resembles fine breadcrumbs. Stir in the superfine sugar and add enough cold water to mix to a firm dough. Wrap in plastic wrap and chill for 15 minutes, until firm enough to roll out.

Preheat the oven to 400°F/200°C. Roll out the dough on a lightly floured counter and use to line a 9-inch/23-cm loose-bottom round tart pan. Prick the bottom with a fork. Chill for 15 minutes.

Place the tart pan on a cookie sheet and line with a sheet of parchment paper and dried beans. Bake blind in the preheated oven for 10 minutes. Remove the paper and beans and bake for an additional 5 minutes. Reduce the oven temperature to 350°F/180°C.

For the filling, place the butter, brown sugar, and corn syrup in a saucepan and heat gently until melted. Remove from the heat and quickly beat in the eggs and vanilla extract.

Coarsely chop the pecans and stir into the mixture. Pour into the tart shell and bake for 35–40 minutes, until the filling is just set. Serve warm or cold.

SERVES 8

pue dough

1¾ cups all-purpose flour, plus extra for dusting

½ cup butter

2 tbsp superfine sugar

a little cold water

filling

5 tbsp butter

scant ½ cup light brown sugar

⅔ cup dark corn syrup

2 extra-large eggs, beaten

1 tsp vanilla extract

1 cup pecans

MISSISSIPPI MUD PIE

SERVES 8

pie dough

1½ cups all-purpose flour, plus extra for dusting

2 tbsp unsweetened cocoa

generous ½ cup unsalted butter

2 tbsp superfine sugar

1–2 tbsp cold water

filling

¾ cup unsalted butter

scant 1¾ cups firmly packed dark brown sugar

4 eggs, lightly beaten

4 tbsp unsweetened cocoa, sifted

5½ oz/150 g semisweet chocolate

1¼ cups light cream

1 tsp chocolate extract

to decorate

scant 2 cups heavy cream, whipped

chocolate flakes and curls

To make the pie dough, sift the flour and cocoa into a mixing bowl. Rub in the butter with your fingertips until the mixture resembles fine breadcrumbs. Stir in the sugar and enough cold water to mix to a soft dough. Wrap the dough in plastic wrap and let chill in the refrigerator for 15 minutes.

Preheat the oven to 375°F/190°C. Roll out the dough on a lightly floured counter and use to line a 9-inch/23-cm loose-bottom round tart pan. Line with parchment paper and fill with dried beans. Bake in the preheated oven for 15 minutes. Remove from the oven and take out the paper and beans. Bake the pastry shell for an additional 10 minutes.

To make the filling, beat the butter and sugar together in a bowl and gradually beat in the eggs with the cocoa. Melt the chocolate in a heatproof bowl set over a saucepan of gently simmering water, then beat it into the mixture with the light cream and the chocolate extract.

Reduce the oven temperature to 325°F/160°C. Pour the mixture into the pastry shell and bake for 45 minutes, or until the filling has set gently.

Let the mud pie cool completely, then transfer it to a serving plate. Cover with the whipped cream. Decorate the pie with chocolate flakes and curls and let chill until ready to serve.

STRAWBERRY TARTLETS

To make the pie dough, sift the flour and confectioners' sugar into a bowl. Chop the butter into small pieces and add to the flour mixture with the egg yolk, mixing with your fingertips and adding a little water, if necessary, to mix to a soft dough. Cover and place in the refrigerator to rest for 15 minutes.

Preheat the oven to 400°F/200°C. Roll out the dough and use to line four 3½-inch/9-cm round tartlet pans. Prick the bottoms with a fork, line with parchment paper, and fill with dried beans, then bake blind in the preheated oven for 10 minutes. Remove the paper and beans and bake for an additional 5 minutes, until golden brown. Remove from the oven and let cool.

For the filling, place the vanilla bean in a saucepan with the milk and set over low heat to steep, without boiling, for 10 minutes. Whisk the egg yolks, sugar, flour, and cornstarch together in a mixing bowl until smooth. Strain the milk into the bowl and whisk until smooth.

Pour the mixture back into the pan and stir over medium heat until boiling. Cook, stirring continuously, for about 2 minutes, until thickened and smooth. Remove from the heat and fold in the whipped cream. Spoon the mixture into the pie shells.

Let cool and set. When the filling has set slightly, top with strawberries, sliced if large, then spoon over a little grape jelly to glaze.

MAKES 4

pie dough
generous 1 cup all-purpose flour

2 tbsp confectioners' sugar

5 tbsp unsalted butter, at room temperature

1 egg yolk

1–2 tbsp water

filling
1 vanilla bean, split

scant 1 cup milk

2 egg yolks

3 tbsp superfine sugar

1 tbsp all-purpose flour

1 tbsp cornstarch

½ cup heavy cream, whipped

3 cups strawberries, hulled

4 tbsp grape jelly, melted

APPLE STRUDEL

Preheat the oven to 375°F/190°C. Line a baking sheet with parchment paper.

Peel and core the apples and chop them into ½-inch/1-cm dice. Toss the apples in a bowl with the lemon juice, golden raisins, cinnamon, nutmeg, and brown sugar.

Lay out a sheet of filo dough, spray with vegetable oil, and lay a second sheet on top. Repeat with a third sheet. Spread over half the apple mixture and roll up lengthwise, tucking in the ends to enclose the filling. Repeat to make a second strudel. Slide onto the baking sheet, spray with oil, and bake in the preheated oven for 15–20 minutes.

To make the sauce, blend the cornstarch in a saucepan with a little hard cider until smooth. Add the remaining cider and heat gently, stirring, until the mixture boils and thickens. Serve the strudel warm or cold, dredged with confectioners' sugar and accompanied by the cider sauce.

SERVES 2–4

8 apples

1 tbsp lemon juice

⅔ cup golden raisins

1 tsp ground cinnamon

½ tsp ground nutmeg

1 tbsp light brown sugar

6 sheets filo dough, thawed if frozen

vegetable oil spray

confectioners' sugar, to serve

sauce

1 tbsp cornstarch

2 cups hard cider

BAKLAVA

MAKES 25

2 cups walnut halves

1¾ cups shelled pistachios

¾ cup blanched almonds

4 tbsp pine nuts

finely grated rind of 2 large
oranges

6 tbsp sesame seeds

1 tbsp sugar

½ tsp ground cinnamon

½ tsp allspice

23 sheets filo dough, thawed
if frozen

1 cup butter, melted,
plus extra for greasing

syrup

3 cups superfine sugar

2 cups water

5 tbsp honey

3 cloves

2 large strips lemon zest

To make the filling, put the walnuts, pistachios, almonds, and pine nuts in a food processor and process gently, until finely chopped but not ground. Transfer the chopped nuts to a bowl and stir in the orange rind, sesame seeds, sugar, cinnamon, and allspice.

Preheat the oven to 325°F/160°C. Grease a 10-inch/25-cm square ovenproof dish, about 2 inches/5 cm deep. With the filo sheets stacked, cut to size using a ruler. Keep the sheets covered with a damp dish towel. Place a sheet of filo on the bottom of the dish and brush with melted butter. Top with seven more sheets, brushing with butter between each layer.

Sprinkle with 1 cup of the filling. Top with three sheets of filo, brushing each one with butter. Continue layering until you have used up all the filo and filling, ending with a top layer of three sheets of filo. Brush with butter.

Using a sharp knife and a ruler, cut the baklava into 2-inch/5-cm squares. Brush again with butter. Bake in the preheated oven for 1 hour.

Meanwhile, put all the syrup ingredients in a saucepan, stirring to dissolve the sugar. Bring to a boil, then simmer for 15 minutes, without stirring, until a thin syrup forms. Let cool.

Remove the baklava from the oven and strain the syrup over the top. Let set in the dish, then remove the squares to serve.

APPLE DANISH

Place the flour in a bowl and rub in 2 tablespoons of the butter. Chill the remaining butter in the freezer until hard but not frozen. Dust with flour and grate coarsely into a bowl. Chill. Stir the salt, yeast, and sugar into the flour mixture. In another bowl, beat the egg with the vanilla extract and water, then add to the flour mixture and mix to form a dough. Knead for 10 minutes on a floured surface, then chill for 10 minutes.

Roll out the dough to 12 x 8 inches/30 x 20 cm and mark it lengthwise into thirds. Sprinkle the grated butter over the top two thirds, leaving a ½–¾-inch/1–2-cm border around the edge. Fold the bottom third of dough over the center, then fold the top third down. Give the dough a quarter turn (so the short edge is nearest you) and roll out as big as the original rectangle. Fold the bottom third up and the top third down again. Wrap in plastic wrap and chill for 30 minutes. Repeat this rolling, folding, and turning four times, chilling well each time. Chill the dough overnight.

Preheat the oven to 400°F/200°C. Grease two baking sheets. For the filling, mix the apples with the lemon rind and 3 tablespoons of the sugar. Roll out the dough into a 16-inch/40-cm square and cut into 16 squares. Pile a little of the apple filling in the center of each square. Brush the edges with milk and fold the corners together into the center over the filling. Place on the prepared baking sheets and chill for about 15 minutes.

Brush with milk and sprinkle with the remaining sugar. Bake in the preheated oven for 10 minutes. Reduce the temperature to 350°F/180°C and bake for an additional 10–15 minutes.

MAKES 16

danish pastry dough

2 cups white bread flour, plus extra for dusting

¾ cup butter, well chilled, plus extra for greasing

¼ tsp salt

¼ oz/7 g active dry yeast

2 tbsp superfine sugar

1 egg, at room temperature

1 tsp vanilla extract

6 tbsp lukewarm water

milk, for glazing

filling

2 baking apples, peeled, cored, and chopped

grated rind of 1 lemon

4 tbsp sugar

DOUBLE CHOCOLATE SWIRLS

Mix together the flour, yeast, sugar, salt, and cinnamon in a large bowl.

Melt the butter in a heatproof bowl set over a saucepan of gently simmering water, then let cool slightly. Whisk in the eggs and milk. Pour into the flour mixture and mix well to form a dough.

Turn out onto a floured counter and knead for 10 minutes, until smooth. Put into a large floured bowl, cover with plastic wrap, and put in a warm place for 1½–2 hours.

When you are ready to make the swirls, take the dough from the bowl and punch down. Preheat the oven to 425°F/220°C and lightly oil two cookie sheets.

Divide the dough into four pieces and roll each piece into a rectangle about 1 inch/2.5 cm thick. Spread each rectangle with the chocolate hazelnut spread and scatter with the chopped chocolate. Roll up each piece from one of the long edges, then cut into six pieces. Place each swirl, cut-side down, on the prepared cookie sheets and brush well with the beaten egg. Bake in the preheated oven for 12–15 minutes and serve warm.

MAKES 24

4½ cups white bread flour, plus extra for dusting

¼ oz/7 g active dry yeast

½ cup superfine sugar

½ tsp salt

1 tsp ground cinnamon

6 tbsp butter

2 large eggs, beaten, plus extra for glazing

1¼ cups milk

oil, for greasing

filling

6 tbsp chocolate hazelnut spread

7 oz/200 g milk chocolate, chopped

CINNAMON ROLLS

MAKES 8

scant 2½ cups self-rising flour, plus extra for dusting

pinch of salt

2 tbsp superfine sugar

1 tsp ground cinnamon

scant ½ cup butter, melted, plus extra for greasing

2 egg yolks

scant 1 cup milk, plus extra for glazing

filling

1 tsp ground cinnamon

¼ cup light brown sugar

2 tbsp superfine sugar

1 tbsp butter, melted

frosting

1 cup confectioners' sugar, sifted

2 tbsp cream cheese, softened

1 tbsp butter, softened

about 2 tbsp boiling water

1 tsp vanilla extract

Preheat the oven to 350°F/180°C. Grease an 8-inch/20-cm round cake pan and line the bottom with parchment paper.

Mix the flour, salt, superfine sugar, and cinnamon together in a bowl. Whisk the butter, egg yolks, and milk together and combine with the dry ingredients to make a soft dough. Turn out onto a large piece of wax paper lightly sprinkled with flour, and roll out to a rectangle measuring 12 x 10 inches/30 x 25 cm.

To make the filling, mix the ingredients together, spread evenly over the dough, and roll up to form a log. Using a sharp knife, cut the dough into eight even-size slices and pack into the prepared pan. Brush gently with extra milk and bake in the preheated oven for 30–35 minutes, or until golden brown. Remove from the oven and let cool for 5 minutes before removing from the pan.

Sift the confectioners' sugar into a large bowl and make a well in the center. Place the cream cheese and butter in the center, pour over the water, and stir to mix. Add extra boiling water, a few drops at a time, until the frosting coats the back of a spoon. Stir in the vanilla extract. Drizzle over the rolls. Serve warm or cold.

CROWN LOAF

Grease a cookie sheet. Sift the flour and salt into a bowl. Stir in the yeast. Rub in the butter with your fingertips. Add the milk and egg and mix to form a dough.

Place the dough in a greased bowl, cover, and stand in a warm place for 40 minutes, until doubled in size. Punch down the dough lightly for 1 minute. Roll out to a rectangle measuring about 12 x 9 inches/30 x 23 cm.

To make the filling, cream together the butter and sugar until light and fluffy. Stir in the hazelnuts, ginger, candied peel, and rum. Spread the filling over the dough, leaving a 1-inch/2.5-cm border.

Roll up the dough, starting from one of the long edges, into a sausage shape. Cut into slices at 2-inch/5-cm intervals and place, cut-side down, in a circle on the cookie sheet with the slices just touching. Cover and stand in a warm place to rise for 30 minutes.

Meanwhile, preheat the oven to 375°F/190°C. Bake the loaf in the preheated oven for 20–30 minutes, or until golden. Mix the confectioners' sugar with enough lemon juice to form a thin frosting.

Let the loaf cool slightly before drizzling with the frosting. Let the frosting set before serving.

SERVES 6

generous 1½ cups white bread flour

½ tsp salt

¼ oz/7 g active dry yeast

2 tbsp butter, cut into small pieces, plus extra for greasing

½ cup tepid milk

1 egg, lightly beaten

filling

4 tbsp butter, softened

¼ cup light brown sugar

2 tbsp chopped hazelnuts

1 tbsp chopped preserved ginger

⅓ cup chopped candied peel

1 tbsp dark rum or cognac

frosting

1 cup confectioners' sugar

1–2 tbsp lemon juice

FRESH CROISSANTS

Preheat the oven to 400°F/200°C. Stir the dry ingredients into a large bowl, make a well in the center, and add the milk. Mix to a soft dough, adding more milk if too dry. Knead on a lightly floured counter for 5–10 minutes, or until smooth and elastic. Place in a large greased bowl, cover, and let rise in a warm place until doubled in size. Meanwhile, place the butter between two sheets of wax paper and flatten with a rolling pin to form a rectangle about ¼ inch/5 mm thick, then let chill.

Knead the dough for 1 minute. Remove the butter from the refrigerator and let soften slightly. Roll out the dough on a well floured counter to 18 x 6 inches/46 x 15 cm. Place the butter in the center, folding up the sides and squeezing the edges together gently. With the short end of the dough toward you, fold the top third down toward the center, then fold the bottom third up. Give the dough a quarter turn, roll out as big as the original rectangle, and fold again. If the butter feels soft, wrap the dough in plastic wrap and let chill. Repeat the rolling process twice more. Cut the dough in half. Roll out one half to ¼ inch/5 mm thick (keep the other half refrigerated). Use a cardboard triangular template, bottom 7 inches/18 cm and sides 8 inches/20 cm, to cut out six triangles. Repeat with the other half of the dough.

Brush the triangles lightly with the glaze. Roll into croissant shapes, starting at the bottom and tucking the point underneath to prevent the croissants from unrolling while cooking. Brush again with the glaze. Place on a baking sheet and let double in size. Bake in the preheated oven for 15–20 minutes, until golden brown.

MAKES 12

1 lb 2 oz/500 g white bread flour, plus extra for dusting

scant ¼ cup superfine sugar

1 tsp salt

2 tsp active dry yeast

1¼ cups lukewarm milk

generous 1¼ cups butter, softened, plus extra for greasing

1 egg, lightly beaten with 1 tbsp milk, for glazing

PAIN AU CHOCOLAT

MAKES 12

¾ cup butter, softened,
  plus extra for greasing

4 cups white bread flour

½ tsp salt

¼ oz/7 g active dry yeast

2 tbsp shortening

1 egg, lightly beaten

1 cup tepid water

1 egg, beaten, for glazing

3½ oz/100 g semisweet chocolate,
  broken into 12 squares

Lightly grease a cookie sheet. Sift the flour and salt into a
mixing bowl and stir in the yeast. Rub in the shortening with
your fingertips. Add the egg and enough of the water to mix to
a soft dough. Knead for about 10 minutes to make a smooth
elastic dough.

Roll out to a 15 x 8-inch/38 x 20-cm rectangle and mark it
vertically into thirds. Divide the butter into three portions and dot
one portion over the first two thirds of the rectangle, leaving a
small border around the edge.

Fold the rectangle into three by first folding the plain part of
the dough over and then the other side. Seal the edges of the
dough by pressing with a rolling pin. Give the dough a quarter-
turn and roll out as big as the original rectangle. Fold again
(without adding butter), then wrap the dough and let chill for
30 minutes.

Repeat this rolling, folding, and turning twice more until all of
the butter has been used, chilling the dough each time. Re-roll
and fold twice more without butter. Chill for a final 30 minutes.

Roll the dough out to 18 x 12 inches/45 x 30 cm and halve
lengthwise. Cut each half into six rectangles and brush with beaten
egg. Place a chocolate square at one end of each rectangle and
roll up to form a sausage. Press the ends together and place,
seam-side down, on the prepared cookie sheet. Cover and let rise
for 40 minutes in a warm place. Preheat the oven to 425°F/220°C.
Brush each pastry roll with egg and bake in the preheated oven for
20–25 minutes, until golden. Serve warm or cold.

CHOCOLATE ÉCLAIRS

Preheat the oven to 400°F/200°C. Lightly grease a cookie sheet.

Place the water in a saucepan, add the butter, and heat gently until the butter melts. Bring to a rolling boil, then remove the pan from the heat and add the flour all at once, beating well until the mixture leaves the sides of the pan and forms a ball. Let cool slightly, then gradually beat in the eggs to form a smooth, glossy mixture. Spoon into a large pastry bag fitted with a ½-inch/1-cm plain tip.

Sprinkle the cookie sheet with water. Pipe éclairs 3 inches/ 7.5 cm long, spaced well apart. Bake in the preheated oven for 30–35 minutes, until crisp and golden. Make a small slit in the side of each éclair to let the steam escape. Let cool on a wire rack.

Meanwhile, make the pastry cream. Whisk the eggs and superfine sugar until thick and creamy, then fold in the cornstarch. Heat the milk in a saucepan until almost boiling and pour onto the egg mixture, whisking. Transfer the egg mixture to the pan and cook over low heat, stirring until thick. Remove the pan from the heat and stir in the vanilla extract. Cover with parchment paper and let cool.

To make the frosting, melt the butter with the milk in a saucepan, remove from the heat, and stir in the cocoa and confectioners' sugar. Split the éclairs lengthwise and pipe in the pastry cream. Spread the frosting over the top of the éclairs. Melt a little white chocolate in a heatproof bowl set over a saucepan of simmering water, then spoon over the chocolate frosting, swirl in, and let set.

MAKES 12

choux pastry
⅔ cup water

5 tbsp butter, cut into small pieces, plus extra for greasing

¾ cup all-purpose flour, sifted

2 eggs

pastry cream
2 eggs, lightly beaten

¼ cup superfine sugar

2 tbsp cornstarch

1¼ cups milk

¼ tsp vanilla extract

frosting
2 tbsp butter

1 tbsp milk

1 tbsp unsweetened cocoa

½ cup confectioners' sugar

1¾ oz/50 g white chocolate, broken into pieces

STRAWBERRY PETITS CHOUX

Sprinkle the gelatin over the water in a heatproof bowl. Let it soften for 2–3 minutes. Place the bowl over a saucepan of gently simmering water and stir until the gelatin dissolves. Remove from the heat.

Place a scant 1 cup of the strawberries in a blender with the ricotta cheese, sugar, and liqueur. Process until blended. Add the gelatin and process briefly. Transfer the mousse to a bowl, cover with plastic wrap, and chill for 1–1½ hours, until set.

Preheat the oven to 425°F/220°C. Line a cookie sheet with parchment paper. To make the petits choux, sift together the flour, cocoa, and salt. Put the butter and water into a heavy-bottom saucepan and heat gently until the butter has melted. Remove the pan from the heat and add the flour, cocoa, and salt all at once, stirring well until the mixture leaves the sides of the pan. Let cool slightly.

Gradually beat the eggs and egg white into the flour paste and continue beating until it is smooth and glossy. Drop 12 rounded tablespoonfuls of the mixture onto the prepared cookie sheet and bake in the preheated oven for 20–25 minutes, until puffed up and crisp. Remove from the oven and make a slit in the side of each petit chou. Return to the oven for 5 minutes. Transfer to a wire rack.

Slice the remaining strawberries. Cut the petits choux in half, divide the mousse and strawberry slices among them, then replace the tops. Dust lightly with confectioners' sugar and place in the refrigerator. Serve within 1½ hours.

MAKES 12

filling and topping

2 tsp powdered gelatin

2 tbsp water

3 cups strawberries, hulled

1 cup ricotta cheese

1 tbsp superfine sugar

2 tsp strawberry-flavored liqueur

confectioners' sugar, for dusting

petits choux

¾ cup all-purpose flour

2 tbsp unsweetened cocoa

pinch of salt

6 tbsp butter

1 cup water

2 eggs, plus 1 egg white, beaten

PROFITEROLES & CHOCOLATE SAUCE

SERVES 4

choux pastry
generous ¾ cup water

5 tbsp butter, plus extra
    for greasing

¾ cup all-purpose flour, sifted

3 eggs, beaten

cream filling
1¼ cups heavy cream

3 tbsp superfine sugar

1 tsp vanilla extract

chocolate sauce
4½ oz/125 g semisweet chocolate,
    broken into small pieces

2½ tbsp butter

6 tbsp water

2 tbsp brandy

Preheat the oven to 400°F/200°C. Grease a large cookie sheet.

To make the pastry, put the water and butter into a saucepan and bring to a boil. Immediately add all the flour, remove the pan from the heat, and stir the mixture into a paste that leaves the sides of the pan clean. Let cool slightly. Beat in enough of the eggs to give the mixture a soft dropping consistency.

Put the mixture into a pastry bag fitted with a ½-inch/1-cm plain tip. Pipe small balls onto the prepared cookie sheet. Bake in the preheated oven for 25 minutes. Remove from the oven. Pierce each ball with a skewer to let the steam escape.

To make the filling, whip the cream, sugar, and vanilla extract together. Cut the pastry balls almost in half, then fill with cream.

To make the sauce, gently melt the chocolate and butter with the water in a heatproof bowl set over a saucepan of gently simmering water, stirring, until smooth. Stir in the brandy. Pile the profiteroles into individual serving dishes or into a pyramid on a raised cake stand. Pour over the sauce and serve.

COOKIES

CHOCOLATE CHIP COOKIES

Preheat the oven to 375°F/190°C. Lightly grease two cookie sheets.

Place all of the ingredients in a large mixing bowl and beat until thoroughly combined.

Place tablespoonfuls of the mixture onto the cookie sheets, spacing them well apart to allow for spreading during cooking.

Bake in the preheated oven for 10–12 minutes, or until the cookies are golden brown.

Using a spatula, transfer the cookies to a wire rack to cool completely.

MAKES 30

1½ cups all-purpose flour

1 tsp baking powder

½ cup soft margarine, plus extra for greasing

½ cup light brown sugar

¼ cup superfine sugar

½ tsp vanilla extract

1 egg

⅔ cup semisweet chocolate chips

MEGA CHIP COOKIES

Preheat the oven to 375°F/190°C. Line two cookie sheets with parchment paper.

Put the butter and sugar into a bowl and mix well with a wooden spoon, then beat in the egg yolk and vanilla extract. Sift together the flour, cocoa, and salt into the mixture, add both kinds of chocolate chips, and stir until thoroughly combined.

Make 12 balls of the mixture, put them on the prepared cookie sheets, spaced well apart, and flatten slightly. Press the pieces of semisweet chocolate into the cookies.

Bake in the preheated oven for 12–15 minutes. Let cool on the cookie sheets for 5–10 minutes, then, using a metal spatula, carefully transfer to wire racks to cool completely.

MAKES 12

1 cup butter, softened

scant ¾ cup superfine sugar

1 egg yolk, lightly beaten

2 tsp vanilla extract

2 cups all-purpose flour

½ cup unsweetened cocoa

pinch of salt

½ cup milk chocolate chips

½ cup white chocolate chips

4 oz/115 g semisweet chocolate, coarsely chopped

CLASSIC OATMEAL COOKIES

MAKES 30

¾ cup butter or margarine, plus extra for greasing

scant 1⅓ cups raw brown sugar

1 egg

4 tbsp water

1 tsp vanilla extract

4⅓ cups rolled oats

1 cup all-purpose flour

1 tsp salt

½ tsp baking soda

Preheat the oven to 350°F/180°C and grease a large cookie sheet.

Cream the butter and sugar together in a large mixing bowl. Beat in the egg, water, and vanilla extract until the mixture is smooth.

In a separate bowl, mix the oats, flour, salt, and baking soda together. Gradually stir the oat mixture into the butter mixture until thoroughly combined.

Put tablespoonfuls of the mixture onto the prepared cookie sheet, making sure they are well spaced. Transfer to the preheated oven and bake for 15 minutes, or until the cookies are golden brown.

Remove the cookies from the oven and place on a wire rack to cool before serving.

TRADITIONAL EASTER COOKIES

Put the butter and sugar into a bowl and mix well with a wooden spoon, then beat in the egg yolk. Sift together the flour, apple pie spice, and salt together into the mixture, add the candied peel and currants, and stir until thoroughly combined. Halve the dough, shape into balls, wrap in plastic wrap, and chill in the refrigerator for 30–60 minutes.

Preheat the oven to 375°F/190°C. Line two cookie sheets with parchment paper.

Unwrap the dough and roll out between two sheets of parchment paper. Stamp out rounds with a 2½-inch/6-cm fluted cookie cutter and put them on the prepared cookie sheets, spaced well apart.

Bake in the preheated oven for 7 minutes, then brush with the egg white and sprinkle with superfine sugar. Return to the oven and bake for an additional 5–8 minutes, until light golden brown. Let cool on the cookie sheets for 5–10 minutes, then, using a metal spatula, carefully transfer to wire racks to cool completely.

MAKES ABOUT 30

1 cup butter, softened

scant ¾ cup superfine sugar, plus extra for sprinkling

1 egg yolk, lightly beaten

2½ cups all-purpose flour

1 tsp apple pie spice

pinch of salt

1 tbsp chopped candied peel

¼ cup currants

1 egg white, lightly beaten

PEANUT BUTTER COOKIES

Preheat the oven to 350°F/180°C, then grease three cookie sheets.

Place the butter and peanut butter in a bowl and beat together. Beat in the superfine sugar and brown sugar, then gradually beat in the egg and vanilla extract.

Sift the flour, baking soda, baking powder, and salt into the bowl and stir in the oats.

Place spoonfuls of the cookie dough onto the cookie sheets, spaced well apart to allow for spreading. Flatten slightly with a fork.

Bake in the preheated oven for 12 minutes, or until lightly browned. Let cool on the cookie sheets for 2 minutes, then transfer to wire racks to cool completely.

MAKES 26

½ cup butter, softened, plus extra for greasing

scant ½ cup crunchy peanut butter

generous ½ cup superfine sugar

generous ½ cup light brown sugar

1 egg, beaten

½ tsp vanilla extract

⅔ cup all-purpose flour

½ tsp baking soda

½ tsp baking powder

pinch of salt

1½ cups rolled oats

SNICKERDOODLES

MAKES ABOUT 40

1 cup butter, softened

scant ¾ cup superfine sugar

2 extra-large eggs, lightly beaten

1 tsp vanilla extract

3½ cups all-purpose flour

1 tsp baking soda

½ tsp freshly grated nutmeg

pinch of salt

½ cup finely chopped pecans

cinnamon coating

1 tbsp superfine sugar

2 tsp ground cinnamon

Put the butter and sugar into a bowl and mix well with a wooden spoon, then beat in the eggs and vanilla extract. Sift the flour, baking soda, nutmeg, and salt together into the mixture, add the pecans, and stir until thoroughly combined. Shape the dough into a ball, wrap in plastic wrap, and chill in the refrigerator for 30–60 minutes.

Preheat the oven to 375°F/190°C. Line two cookie sheets with parchment paper.

For the coating, mix together the superfine sugar and cinnamon in a shallow dish. Scoop up tablespoons of the cookie dough and roll into balls. Roll each ball in the cinnamon mixture to coat and put on the prepared cookie sheets, spaced well apart.

Bake in the preheated oven for 10–12 minutes, until golden brown. Let cool on the cookie sheets for 5–10 minutes, then, using a metal spatula, carefully transfer to wire racks to cool completely.

GINGERSNAPS

Preheat the oven to 325°F/160°C. Lightly grease several cookie sheets.

Sift together the flour, salt, sugar, ground ginger, and baking soda into a large mixing bowl.

Heat the butter and corn syrup together in a saucepan over very low heat until the butter has melted.

Let the butter mixture cool slightly, then pour it onto the dry ingredients. Add the egg and orange rind and mix together thoroughly.

Using your hands, carefully shape the dough into 30 even-size balls. Place the balls on the prepared cookie sheets, spaced well apart, then flatten them slightly with your fingers.

Bake in the preheated oven for 15–20 minutes. Carefully transfer the cookies to a wire rack to cool and crisp.

MAKES 30

2½ cups self-rising flour

pinch of salt

1 cup superfine sugar

1 tbsp ground ginger

1 tsp baking soda

½ cup butter, plus extra for greasing

¼ cup dark corn syrup

1 egg, lightly beaten

1 tsp grated orange rind

SHORTBREAD

Preheat the oven to 300°F/150°C. Grease an 8-inch/20-cm fluted round tart pan.

Mix together the flour, salt, and sugar. Rub the butter into the dry ingredients. Continue to work the mixture until it forms a soft dough. Make sure you do not overwork the shortbread or it will be tough, not crumbly as it should be.

Lightly press the dough into the prepared tart pan. If you don't have a fluted pan, roll out the dough on a lightly floured board, place on a cookie sheet, and pinch the edges to form a scalloped pattern.

Mark into eight pieces with a knife. Prick all over with a fork and bake in the center of the oven for 45–50 minutes, until the shortbread is firm and just colored.

Let cool in the pan and sprinkle with the sugar. Cut into portions and transfer to a wire rack.

MAKES 8

scant 1½ cups all-purpose flour, plus extra for dusting

pinch of salt

¼ cup superfine sugar, plus extra for sprinkling

¾ cup butter, cut into small pieces, plus extra for greasing

CITRUS CRESCENTS

MAKES ABOUT 25

⅓ cup butter, softened, plus extra for greasing

⅓ cup superfine sugar

1 egg, separated

1¾ cups all-purpose flour, plus extra for dusting

grated rind of 1 orange

grated rind of 1 lemon

grated rind of 1 lime

2–3 tbsp orange juice

Preheat the oven to 400°F/200°C. Lightly grease two cookie sheets.

In a mixing bowl, cream together the butter and sugar until light and fluffy, then gradually beat in the egg yolk.

Sift the flour into the creamed mixture and mix until evenly combined. Add the orange rind, lemon rind, and lime rind to the mixture with enough of the orange juice to make a soft dough.

Roll out the dough on a lightly floured counter. Stamp out rounds using a 3-inch/7.5-cm cookie cutter. Make crescent shapes by cutting away one quarter of each round. Re-roll the trimmings to make about 25 crescents in total.

Place the crescents on the prepared cookie sheets. Prick the surface of each crescent with a fork. Lightly whisk the egg white in a small bowl and brush it over the cookies.

Bake in the preheated oven for 12–15 minutes. Let the cookies cool on a wire rack before serving.

VANILLA HEARTS

Preheat the oven to 350°F/180°C, then lightly grease a cookie sheet.

Sift the flour into a large bowl. Add the butter and rub it in with your fingertips until the mixture resembles fine breadcrumbs. Stir in the sugar and vanilla extract and mix together to form a firm dough.

Roll out the dough on a lightly floured counter to a thickness of ½ inch/1 cm. Stamp out 12 hearts with a heart-shaped cookie cutter measuring 2 inches/5 cm across. Arrange the hearts on the prepared cookie sheet.

Bake in the preheated oven for 15–20 minutes, or until just colored. Transfer to a wire rack and let cool completely. Dust with a little superfine sugar just before serving.

MAKES 12

1½ cups all-purpose flour, plus extra for dusting

scant ¾ cup butter, cut into small pieces, plus extra for greasing

1⅛ cups superfine sugar, plus extra for dusting

1 tsp vanilla extract

JELLY RINGS

Put the butter and superfine sugar into a bowl and mix well with a wooden spoon, then beat in the egg yolk and vanilla extract. Sift the flour and salt together into the mixture and stir until thoroughly combined. Halve the dough, shape into balls, wrap in plastic wrap, and chill in the refrigerator for 30–60 minutes.

Preheat the oven to 375°F/190°C. Line two cookie sheets with parchment paper.

Unwrap the dough and roll out between two sheets of parchment paper. Stamp out cookies with a 2¾-inch/7-cm fluted round cutter and put half of them on one of the prepared cookie trays, spaced well apart. Using a 1½-inch/4-cm plain round cutter, stamp out the centers of the remaining cookies and remove. Put the cookie rings on the other cookie sheet, spaced well apart.

Bake in the preheated oven for 7 minutes, then brush the cookie rings with beaten egg white and sprinkle with superfine sugar. Bake for 5–8 minutes more, until light golden brown. Let cool on the cookie sheets for 5–10 minutes, then, using a metal spatula, carefully transfer to wire racks to cool completely.

To make the filling, beat the butter and confectioners' sugar together in a bowl until smooth and combined. Spread the buttercream over the whole cookies and top with a little jelly. Place the cookie rings on top and press gently together.

MAKES ABOUT 15

1 cup butter, softened

scant ¾ cup superfine sugar, plus extra for sprinkling

1 egg yolk, lightly beaten

2 tsp vanilla extract

2½ cups all-purpose flour

pinch of salt

1 egg white, lightly beaten

filling

¼ cup butter, softened

scant 1 cup confectioners' sugar

5 tbsp strawberry jelly or raspberry jelly, warmed

GINGERBREAD PEOPLE

MAKES 20

3½ cups all-purpose flour, plus extra for dusting

2 tsp ground ginger

1 tsp ground allspice

2 tsp baking soda

½ cup butter, plus extra for greasing

generous ⅓ cup dark corn syrup

generous ½ cup light brown sugar

1 egg, beaten

to decorate

currants

candied cherries

generous ¾ cup confectioners' sugar

3–4 tsp water

Preheat the oven to 325°F/160°C, then grease three large cookie sheets.

Sift the flour, ginger, allspice, and baking soda into a large bowl. Place the butter, corn syrup, and brown sugar in a saucepan over low heat and stir until melted. Pour onto the dry ingredients and add the egg. Mix together to make a dough. The dough will be sticky to start with, but will become firmer as it cools.

Roll out the dough on a lightly floured work counter to about ⅛-inch/3-mm thick and stamp out gingerbread people shapes. Place on the prepared cookie sheets. Re-knead and re-roll the trimmings and cut out more shapes. Decorate with currants for eyes and pieces of candied cherry for mouths. Bake in the preheated oven for 15–20 minutes, until firm and lightly browned.

Remove from the oven and let cool on the cookie sheets for a few minutes, then transfer to wire racks to cool completely.

Mix the confectioners' sugar with the water to a thick consistency. Place the frosting in a small pastry bag fitted with a plain tip and use to pipe buttons or bows onto the cooled cookies.

CHOCOLATE DOMINOES

Put the butter and sugar into a bowl and mix well with a wooden spoon, then beat in the egg yolk and vanilla extract. Sift the flour, cocoa, and a pinch of salt together into the mixture, add the coconut, and stir until thoroughly combined. Halve the dough, shape into balls, wrap in plastic wrap, and chill in the refrigerator for 30–60 minutes.

Preheat the oven to 375°F/190°C. Line two cookie sheets with parchment paper.

Unwrap the dough and roll out between two sheets of parchment paper. Stamp out cookies with a 3½-inch/9-cm plain square cutter, then cut them in half to make rectangles. Place them on the prepared cookie sheets and, using a knife, make a line across the center of each without cutting through. Arrange the chocolate chips on top of the cookies to look like dominoes, pressing them in gently.

Bake in the preheated oven for 10–15 minutes, until golden brown. Let cool on the cookie sheets for 5–10 minutes, then, using a metal spatula, carefully transfer to wire racks to cool completely.

MAKES 28

1 cup butter, softened

scant ¾ cup superfine sugar

1 egg yolk, lightly beaten

2 tsp vanilla extract

2¼ cups all-purpose flour

¼ cup unsweetened cocoa

    pinch of salt

⅓ cup dry unsweetened coconut

scant ⅓ cup white chocolate chips

CHECKERBOARD COOKIES

MAKES ABOUT 20

1 cup butter, softened
scant ¾ cup superfine sugar
1 egg yolk, lightly beaten
2 tsp vanilla extract
2½ cups all-purpose flour
pinch of salt
1 tsp ground ginger
1 tbsp finely grated orange rind
1 tbsp unsweetened cocoa, sifted
1 egg white, lightly beaten

Put the butter and sugar into a bowl and mix well with a wooden spoon, then beat in the egg yolk and vanilla extract. Sift the flour and salt together into the mixture and stir until thoroughly combined.

Divide the dough in half. Add the ginger and orange rind to one half and mix well. Shape the dough into a log 6 inches/15 cm long. Flatten the sides and top to square off the log to 2 inches/5 cm high. Wrap in plastic wrap and chill in the refrigerator for 30–60 minutes. Add the cocoa to the other half of the dough and mix well. Shape into a flattened log exactly the same size as the first one, wrap in plastic wrap, and chill in the refrigerator for 30–60 minutes.

Unwrap the dough and cut each flattened log lengthwise into three slices. Cut each slice lengthwise into three strips. Brush the strips with egg white and stack them in threes, alternating the colors, so they are the same shape as the original logs. Wrap in plastic wrap and chill in the refrigerator for 30–60 minutes.

Preheat the oven to 375°F/190°C. Line two cookie sheets with parchment paper.

Unwrap the logs and cut into slices with a sharp serrated knife. Put the cookies on the prepared cookie sheets, spaced well apart. Bake in the preheated oven for 12–15 minutes, until firm. Let cool on the cookie sheets for 5–10 minutes, then, using a metal spatula, carefully transfer to wire racks to cool completely.

CHOCOLATE COOKIE SANDWICHES

MAKES ABOUT 15

1 cup butter, softened

scant ¾ cup superfine sugar

2 tsp finely grated orange rind

1 egg yolk, lightly beaten

2 tsp vanilla extract

2¼ cups all-purpose flour

¼ cup unsweetened cocoa

pinch of salt

3½ oz/100 g semisweet chocolate, finely chopped

chocolate filling

½ cup heavy cream

7 oz/200 g white chocolate, broken into pieces

1 tsp orange extract

Preheat the oven to 375°F/190°C. Line two cookie sheets with parchment paper.

Put the butter, sugar, and orange rind into a bowl and mix well with a wooden spoon, then beat in the egg yolk and vanilla extract. Sift the flour, cocoa, and salt together into the mixture, add the chopped chocolate, and stir until thoroughly combined.

Scoop up tablespoons of the dough, roll into balls, and put on the prepared cookie sheets, spaced well apart. Gently flatten and smooth the tops with the back of a spoon.

Bake in the preheated oven for 10–15 minutes, until light golden brown. Let cool on the cookie sheets for 5–10 minutes, then, using a metal spatula, carefully transfer to wire racks to cool completely.

To make the filling, bring the cream to a boil in a small saucepan, then remove the saucepan from the heat. Stir in the chocolate until the mixture is smooth, then stir in the orange extract. When the mixture is completely cool, use to sandwich the cookies together in pairs.

CHOCOLATE MINT COOKIE SANDWICHES

Put the butter and sugar into a bowl and mix well with a wooden spoon, then beat in the egg yolk and vanilla extract. Sift the flour, cocoa, and salt together into the mixture, add the cherries, and stir until thoroughly combined. Halve the dough, shape into balls, wrap in plastic wrap, and chill in the refrigerator for 30–60 minutes.

Preheat the oven to 375°F/190°C. Line two cookie sheets with parchment paper.

Unwrap the dough and roll out between two sheets of parchment paper. Stamp out cookies with a 2½-inch/6-cm plain square cutter and put them on the prepared cookie sheets, spaced well apart.

Bake in the preheated oven for 10–15 minutes, until firm. Immediately place an after-dinner mint on top of half the cookies, then cover with the remaining cookies. Press down gently and let cool.

Melt the semisweet chocolate in a heatproof bowl set over a saucepan of gently simmering water. Remove from the heat and let cool. Put the cookies on a wire rack over a sheet of parchment paper. Spoon the semisweet chocolate over them, then tap the rack to level the surface and let set. Melt the white chocolate in a heatproof bowl set over a saucepan of barely simmering water. Remove from the heat and let cool. Pipe or drizzle it over the cookies, then let set.

MAKES ABOUT 15

1 cup butter, softened

scant ¾ cup superfine sugar

1 egg yolk, lightly beaten

2 tsp vanilla extract

2¼ cups all-purpose flour

½ cup unsweetened cocoa

pinch of salt

⅓ cup candied cherries, finely chopped

15 after-dinner mint thins

chocolate coating

4 oz/115 g semisweet chocolate, broken into pieces

2 oz/55 g white chocolate, broken into pieces

FROSTED CHERRY RINGS

Preheat the oven to 400°F/200°C. Lightly grease two cookie sheets.

Cream together the butter and superfine sugar until pale and fluffy. Beat in the egg yolk and lemon rind. Sift in the flour, stir, then add the candied cherries, mixing with your hands to a soft dough.

Roll out the dough on a lightly floured counter to about ¼ inch/5 mm thick. Stamp out rounds with a 3¼-inch/8-cm cookie cutter. Cut out the center of each with a 1-inch/2.5-cm cutter and place the rings on the prepared cookie sheets. Re-roll any trimmings and cut out more cookies.

Bake in the preheated oven for 12–15 minutes, until firm and golden brown. Let cool on the cookie sheets for 2 minutes, then transfer to a wire rack to finish cooling.

Mix the confectioners' sugar to a smooth paste with the lemon juice. Drizzle over the cookies and let set.

MAKES ABOUT 18

½ cup unsalted butter, plus extra for greasing

scant ½ cup superfine sugar

1 egg yolk

finely grated rind of ½ lemon

1¾ cups all-purpose flour, plus extra for dusting

¼ cup candied cherries, finely chopped

frosting

¾ cup confectioners' sugar

1½ tbsp lemon juice

VIENNESE FINGERS

MAKES ABOUT 16

scant ½ cup unsalted butter, plus
   extra for greasing

2 tbsp superfine sugar

½ tsp vanilla extract

scant 1 cup self-rising flour

3½ oz/100 g semisweet chocolate

Preheat the oven to 325°F/160°C. Lightly grease two cookie sheets.

Place the butter, sugar, and vanilla extract in a bowl and cream
together until pale and fluffy. Stir in the flour, mixing evenly to a
fairly stiff dough.

Place the mixture in a pastry bag fitted with a large star tip and
pipe about 16 bars, each 2½ inches/6 cm long, onto the prepared
cookie sheets.

Bake in the preheated oven for 10–15 minutes, until pale golden.
Cool for 2–3 minutes on the cookie sheets, then lift carefully onto a
cooling rack with a spatula to finish cooling.

Place the chocolate in a small heatproof bowl over a saucepan
of gently simmering water until melted. Remove from the heat.
Dip the ends of each cookie into the chocolate to coat, then place
on a sheet of parchment paper and let set.

BRANDY SNAPS

Preheat the oven to 325°F/160°C. Line three large cookie sheets with parchment paper.

Place the butter, sugar, and corn syrup in a saucepan and heat gently over low heat, stirring occasionally, until melted. Remove from the heat and let cool slightly. Sift the flour and ginger into the pan and beat until smooth, then stir in the brandy and the lemon rind.

Drop small spoonfuls of the mixture onto the prepared cookie sheets, allowing plenty of room for spreading. Bake one cookie sheet at a time in the preheated oven for 10–12 minutes, or until golden brown.

Remove the first cookie sheet from the oven and let cool for about 30 seconds, then lift each round with a spatula and wrap around the handle of a wooden spoon. If the brandy snaps start to become too firm to wrap, return them to the oven for about 30 seconds to soften again. When the brandy snaps are firm, remove from the spoon handles and finish cooling on a wire rack. Repeat with the remaining cookie sheets.

For the filling, whip the cream with the brandy, if using, and confectioners' sugar until thick. Just before serving, pipe the cream mixture into each end of the brandy snaps.

MAKES ABOUT 20

⅓ cup unsalted butter

scant ½ cup superfine sugar

3 tbsp dark corn syrup

¾ cup all-purpose flour

1 tsp ground ginger

1 tbsp brandy

finely grated rind of ½ lemon

filling

⅔ cup heavy cream

1 tbsp brandy (optional)

1 tbsp confectioners' sugar

PISTACHIO & ALMOND TUILES

Preheat the oven to 325°F/160°C. Line two cookie sheets with parchment paper.

Whisk the egg white lightly with the sugar, then stir in the flour, pistachios, ground almonds, almond extract, and butter, mixing to a soft paste.

Place walnut-size spoonfuls of the mixture on the prepared cookie sheets and use the back of the spoon to spread as thinly as possible. Bake in the preheated oven for 10–15 minutes, until pale golden.

Quickly lift each cookie with a spatula and place over the side of a rolling pin to shape into a curve. When set, transfer to a wire rack to cool.

MAKES 12

1 egg white

generous ¼ cup superfine sugar

¼ cup all-purpose flour

¼ cup pistachios, finely chopped

¼ cup ground almonds

½ tsp almond extract

3 tbsp unsalted butter, melted and cooled

MINI FLORENTINES

MAKES 40

6 tbsp butter, plus extra
 for greasing

1/3 cup superfine sugar

2 tbsp golden raisins or raisins

2 tbsp chopped candied cherries

2 tbsp chopped preserved ginger

1 oz/25 g sunflower seeds

3/4 cup slivered almonds

2 tbsp heavy cream

6 oz/175 g semisweet or milk
 chocolate, broken into pieces

Preheat the oven to 350°F/180°C. Line two cookie sheets with parchment paper.

Place the butter in a small saucepan and heat gently until melted. Add the sugar, stir until dissolved, then bring the mixture to a boil. Remove from the heat and stir in the golden raisins, candied cherries, preserved ginger, sunflower seeds, and almonds. Mix well, then beat in the cream.

Place small teaspoons of the mixture onto the prepared cookie sheet, allowing plenty of space for the mixture to spread during baking. Bake in the preheated oven for 10–12 minutes, or until light golden in color.

Remove from the oven and, while still hot, use a round cookie cutter to pull in the edges to form perfect circles. Let cool and crisp before removing from the cookie sheet.

Put the chocolate in a heatproof bowl set over a saucepan of gently simmering water and stir until melted. Spread most of the chocolate onto a sheet of parchment paper. When the chocolate is on the point of setting, place the cookies flat-side down on the chocolate and let it harden completely.

Cut around the florentines and remove from the parchment paper. Spread the remaining melted chocolate on the coated side of the florentines and use a fork to mark waves in the chocolate. Let set.

ALMOND BISCOTTI

Preheat the oven to 350°F/180°C, then lightly dust a cookie sheet with flour.

Sift the flour, baking powder, and salt into a bowl. Add the sugar, eggs, and orange zest and mix to a dough. Knead in the almonds.

Roll out the dough into a ball, cut in half, and roll out each portion into a log about 1½ inches/4 cm in diameter. Place on the prepared cookie sheet and bake in the preheated oven for 10 minutes. Remove from the oven and let them cool for 5 minutes.

Using a serrated knife, cut the logs into ½ inch/1 cm thick diagonal slices. Arrange the slices on the cookie sheet and return to the oven for 15 minutes, or until slightly golden. Transfer to a wire rack to cool and crisp.

MAKES 20–24

1¾ cups all-purpose flour, plus extra for dusting

1 tsp baking powder

pinch of salt

¾ cup superfine sugar

2 eggs, beaten

finely grated zest of 1 orange

½ cup whole blanched almonds, lightly toasted

LADIES KISSES

Cream the butter and sugar together until pale and fluffy. Beat in the egg yolk, then beat in the ground almonds and flour. Continue beating until thoroughly mixed. Shape the dough into a ball, wrap in plastic wrap, and chill in the refrigerator for 1½–2 hours.

Preheat the oven to 325°F/160°C. Line three cookie sheets with parchment paper.

Unwrap the dough, break off walnut-size pieces, and roll them into balls between the palms of your hands. Place the dough balls on the prepared cookie sheets, allowing space for the cookies to spread during cooking. Bake in the preheated oven for 20–25 minutes, until golden. Carefully transfer the cookies, still on the parchment paper, to wire racks to cool.

Melt the chocolate in a heatproof bowl set over a saucepan of gently simmering water. Remove the cookies from the parchment paper. Spread the melted chocolate on the flat sides and sandwich them together in pairs. Return to the wire racks to cool.

MAKES 20

2 cups unsalted butter

½ cup superfine sugar

1 egg yolk

1 cup ground almonds

1¼ cups all-purpose flour

2 oz/55 g semisweet chocolate, broken into pieces

LEBKUCHEN

MAKES 60

3 eggs

1 cup superfine sugar

½ cup all-purpose flour

2 tsp unsweetened cocoa

1 tsp ground cinnamon

½ tsp ground cardamom

¼ tsp ground cloves

¼ tsp ground nutmeg

generous 1 cup ground almonds

scant ⅓ cup chopped candied peel

to decorate

4 oz/115 g semisweet chocolate

4 oz/115 g white chocolate

sugar crystals

Preheat the oven to 350°F/180°C. Line several cookie sheets with parchment paper.

Put the eggs and sugar in a heatproof bowl set over a saucepan of gently simmering water. Whisk until thick and foamy. Remove the bowl from the pan and continue to whisk for 2 minutes.

Sift the flour, cocoa, cinnamon, cardamom, cloves, and nutmeg into the bowl and stir in with the ground almonds and candied peel. Drop generous teaspoonfuls of the cookie dough onto the prepared cookie sheets, spreading them gently into smooth mounds.

Bake in the preheated oven for 15–20 minutes, until light brown and slightly soft to the touch. Cool on the cookie sheets for 10 minutes, then transfer to wire racks to cool completely.

Put the semisweet and white chocolate in two separate heatproof bowls set over two saucepans of gently simmering water until melted. Dip half the cookies in the melted semisweet chocolate and half in the white chocolate. Sprinkle with sugar crystals and let set.

BREAD & SAVORY

CRUSTY WHITE BREAD

MAKES 1 LOAF

1 egg

1 egg yolk

³⁄₄–1 cup lukewarm water

4½ cups white bread flour, plus extra for dusting

1½ tsp salt

2 tsp superfine sugar

1 tsp active dry yeast

2 tbsp butter, diced

vegetable oil, for brushing

Lightly beat together the egg and egg yolk in a measuring cup. Stir in enough of the lukewarm water to make up to 1¼ cups.

Sift the flour and salt together into a bowl and stir in the sugar and yeast. Add the butter and rub it in with your fingertips until the mixture resembles breadcrumbs. Make a well in the center, pour in the egg mixture, and stir well with a wooden spoon until the dough begins to come together, then knead with your hands until it leaves the side of the bowl.

Turn out onto a lightly floured counter and knead well for about 10 minutes, until smooth and elastic. Brush a bowl with oil. Shape the dough into a ball, put it into the bowl, and cover with a damp dish towel. Let rise in a warm place for 1–2 hours, until the dough has doubled in volume.

Brush a 7½ x 4½ x 3½-inch/19 x 12 x 9-cm loaf pan with oil. Turn out the dough onto a lightly floured counter, punch down with your fist, and knead for 1 minute. With lightly floured hands, shape the dough into a rectangle the same length as the pan and flatten slightly. Fold it lengthwise into three and place in the prepared pan, seam-side down. Cover with a damp dish towel and let rise in a warm place for 30 minutes, until the dough has reached the top of the pan.

Preheat the oven to 425°F/220°C. Bake the loaf in the preheated oven for 30 minutes, until it has shrunk from the sides of the pan, is golden brown, and sounds hollow when tapped on the bottom with your knuckles. Turn out onto a wire rack to cool.

WHOLE WHEAT HARVEST BREAD

Sift the flour and salt together into a bowl, add the bran from the sifter, and stir in the milk, sugar, and yeast. Make a well in the center and pour in the oil and lukewarm water. Stir well with a wooden spoon until the dough begins to come together, then knead with your hands until it leaves the side of the bowl. Turn out onto a lightly floured counter and knead well for about 10 minutes, until smooth and elastic.

Brush a bowl with oil. Shape the dough into a ball, put it into the bowl, and cover with a damp dish towel. Let rise in a warm place for 1 hour, until the dough has doubled in volume.

Brush a 6½ x 4¼ x 3¼-inch/17 x 11 x 8-cm loaf pan with oil. Turn out the dough onto a lightly floured counter, punch down with your fist, and knead for 1 minute. With lightly floured hands, shape the dough into a rectangle the same length as the pan and flatten slightly. Fold it lengthwise into three and place in the prepared pan, seam-side down. Cover with a damp dish towel and let rise in a warm place for 30 minutes, until the dough has reached the top of the pan.

Preheat the oven to 425°F/220°C. Bake the loaf in the preheated oven for about 30 minutes, until it has shrunk from the sides of the pan, the crust is golden brown, and it sounds hollow when tapped on the bottom with your knuckles. Turn out onto a wire rack to cool.

MAKES 1 LOAF

- 2 cups whole wheat bread flour, plus extra for dusting
- 1 tsp salt
- 1 tbsp nonfat dry milk
- 2 tbsp light brown sugar
- 1 tsp active dry yeast
- 1½ tbsp vegetable oil, plus extra for brushing
- ¾ cup lukewarm water

MIXED SEED BREAD

MAKES 1 LOAF

3¼ cups white bread flour, plus extra for dusting

scant 1¼ cups rye flour

1½ tsp salt

1½ tbsp nonfat dry milk

1 tbsp light brown sugar

1 tsp active dry yeast

1½ tbsp sunflower oil, plus extra for brushing

2 tsp lemon juice

1¼ cups lukewarm water

1 tsp caraway seeds

½ tsp poppy seeds

½ tsp sesame seeds

topping

1 egg white

1 tbsp water

1 tbsp sunflower or pumpkin seeds

Sift both types of flour and the salt together into a bowl and stir in the milk, sugar, and yeast. Make a well in the center and pour in the oil, lemon juice, and lukewarm water. Add the seeds. Stir well with a wooden spoon until the dough begins to come together, then knead with your hands until it leaves the side of the bowl. Turn out onto a lightly floured counter and knead well for about 10 minutes, until smooth and elastic.

Brush a bowl with oil. Shape the dough into a ball, put it into the bowl, and cover with a damp dish towel. Let rise in a warm place for 1 hour, until the dough has doubled in volume.

Brush a 9 x 5 x 3-inch/23 x 13 x 8-cm loaf pan with oil. Turn out the dough onto a lightly floured counter, punch down with your fist, and knead for 1 minute. With lightly floured hands, shape the dough into a rectangle the same length as the pan and flatten slightly. Fold it lengthwise into three and place in the pan, seam-side down. Cover with a damp dish towel and let rise in a warm place for 30 minutes, until the dough has reached the top of the pan.

Preheat the oven to 425°F/220°C. For the topping, lightly beat the egg white with the water in a bowl. Brush the top of the loaf with egg white glaze and sprinkle with the seeds. Bake in the preheated oven for 30 minutes, until golden brown and the loaf sounds hollow when tapped on the bottom with your knuckles. Turn out onto a wire rack to cool.

BRAIDED POPPY SEED BREAD

Sift the flour and salt together into a bowl and stir in the milk, sugar, and yeast. Make a well in the center and pour in the lukewarm water and oil. Stir well with a wooden spoon until the dough begins to come together. Add the poppy seeds and knead with your hands until they are fully incorporated and the dough leaves the side of the bowl. Turn out onto a lightly floured counter and knead well for about 10 minutes, until smooth and elastic.

Brush a bowl with oil. Shape the dough into a ball, put it into the bowl, and cover with a damp dish towel. Let rise in a warm place for 1 hour, until the dough has doubled in volume.

Brush a cookie sheet with oil. Turn out the dough onto a lightly floured surface, punch down with your fist, and knead for 1–2 minutes. Divide the dough into three equal pieces and shape each into a rope 10–12 inches/25–30 cm long. Place the ropes side by side and press them together at one end. Braid the dough, pinch the other ends together, and tuck underneath. Put the loaf on the prepared cookie sheet. Cover the cookie sheet with a damp dish towel and let rise in a warm place for 30 minutes.

Preheat the oven to 400°F/200°C. To make the topping, beat the egg yolk with the milk and sugar. Brush the egg glaze over the top of the loaf and sprinkle with the poppy seeds. Bake in the preheated oven for 30–35 minutes, until golden brown and the loaf sounds hollow when tapped on the bottom with your knuckles. Transfer to a wire rack to cool.

MAKES 1 LOAF

- 2 cups white bread flour, plus extra for dusting
- 1 tsp salt
- 2 tbsp nonfat dry milk
- 1½ tbsp superfine sugar
- 1 tsp active dry yeast
- ¾ cup lukewarm water
- 2 tbsp vegetable oil, plus extra for brushing
- 5 tbsp poppy seeds

topping
- 1 egg yolk
- 1 tbsp milk
- 1 tbsp superfine sugar
- 2 tbsp poppy seeds

RYE BREAD

Sift the flours and salt together into a bowl. Add the sugar and yeast and stir to mix. Make a well in the center and pour in the lukewarm water and oil. Stir with a wooden spoon until the dough begins to come together, then knead with your hands until it leaves the side of the bowl. Turn out onto a lightly floured counter and knead for 10 minutes, until elastic and smooth.

Brush a bowl with oil. Shape the dough into a ball, put it into the bowl, and cover with a damp dish towel. Let rise in a warm place for 2 hours, until the dough has doubled in volume.

Brush a cookie sheet with oil. Turn out the dough onto a lightly floured counter and punch down with your fist, then knead for an additional 10 minutes. Shape the dough into a ball, put it on the prepared cookie sheet, and cover with a damp dish towel. Let rise in a warm place for an additional 40 minutes, until the dough has doubled in volume.

Meanwhile, preheat the oven to 375°F/190°C. Beat the egg white with 1 tablespoon of water in a bowl. Bake in the preheated oven for 20 minutes, then remove from the oven, and brush the top with the egg white glaze. Return to the oven and bake for an additional 20 minutes. Brush the top of the loaf with the glaze again and return to the oven for 20–30 minutes, until the crust is a rich brown color and the loaf sounds hollow when tapped on the bottom with your knuckles. Transfer to a wire rack to cool.

MAKES 1 LARGE LOAF

- 4 cups rye flour
- 2 cups white bread flour, plus extra for dusting
- 2 tsp salt
- 2 tsp light brown sugar
- 1½ tsp active dry yeast
- scant 2 cups lukewarm water
- 2 tsp vegetable oil, plus extra for brushing
- 1 egg white

WALNUT & SEED BREAD

MAKES 2 LARGE LOAVES

- 4 cups whole wheat flour
- 4 cups multigrain flour
- 1 cup white bread flour, plus extra for dusting
- 2 tbsp sesame seeds
- 2 tbsp sunflower seeds
- 2 tbsp poppy seeds
- 1 cup chopped walnuts
- 2 tsp salt
- ½ oz/15 g active dry yeast
- 2 tbsp olive oil or walnut oil
- 3 cups lukewarm water
- 1 tbsp melted butter or oil, for greasing

In a mixing bowl, combine the flours, seeds, walnuts, salt, and yeast. Add the oil and lukewarm water and stir well to form a soft dough. Turn out the dough onto a lightly floured counter and knead well for 5–7 minutes. The dough should have a smooth appearance and feel elastic.

Return the dough to the bowl, cover with a clean dish towel or plastic wrap, and let stand in a warm place for 1–1½ hours to rise.

When the dough has doubled in size, turn it out onto a lightly floured counter and knead again for 1 minute.

Grease two 9 x 5 x 3-inch/23 x 13 x 8-cm loaf pans well with melted butter or oil. Divide the dough in two. Shape one piece the length of the pan and three times the width. Fold the dough into three lengthwise and place in one of the pans with the seam underneath. Repeat with the other piece of dough.

Cover and let rise again in a warm place for about 30 minutes, until the bread is well risen above the pans. Meanwhile, preheat the oven to 450°F/230°C.

Bake in the center of the preheated oven for 25–30 minutes. If the loaves are getting too brown, reduce the temperature to 425°F/220°C. Test that the bread is cooked by tapping on the bottom with your knuckles—it should sound hollow. Transfer to a wire rack to cool.

IRISH SODA BREAD

Preheat the oven to 425°F/220°C. Brush a cookie sheet with oil.

Sift the flour, salt, and baking soda together into a bowl. Make a well in the center and pour in most of the buttermilk. Mix well, first with a wooden spoon and then with your hands. The dough should be very soft but not too wet. If necessary, add the remaining buttermilk.

Turn out the dough onto a lightly floured counter and knead lightly and briefly. Shape into an 8-inch/20-cm round. Put the loaf onto the prepared cookie sheet and cut a cross in the top with a sharp knife.

Bake in the preheated oven for 25–30 minutes, until golden brown and the loaf sounds hollow when tapped on the bottom with your knuckles. Transfer to a wire rack to cool slightly and serve warm.

MAKES 1 LOAF

vegetable oil, for brushing

4 cups all-purpose flour, plus extra for dusting

1 tsp salt

1 tsp baking soda

1¾ cups buttermilk

CORN BREAD

Preheat the oven to 400°F/200°C. Brush an 8-inch/20-cm square cake pan with oil.

Sift the flour, salt, and baking powder together into a bowl. Add the sugar and cornmeal and stir to mix. Add the butter, then rub in with your fingertips until the mixture resembles breadcrumbs.

Lightly beat the eggs with the milk and cream in a bowl, then stir into the cornmeal mixture until thoroughly combined.

Spoon the mixture into the prepared pan and smooth the surface. Bake in the preheated oven for 30–35 minutes, until a skewer inserted into the center of the loaf comes out clean. Remove the pan from the oven and let the bread cool for 5–10 minutes, then cut into squares and serve warm.

MAKES 1 LOAF

vegetable oil, for brushing

1½ cups all-purpose flour

1 tsp salt

4 tsp baking powder

1 tsp superfine sugar

2½ cups yellow cornmeal

½ cup butter, softened, diced

4 eggs

1 cup milk

3 tbsp heavy cream

CILANTRO & GARLIC NAAN

MAKES 3

2½ cups white bread flour, plus extra for dusting

1 tsp salt

1 tbsp ground coriander

1 garlic clove, very finely chopped

1 tsp active dry yeast

2 tsp honey

scant ½ cup lukewarm water

4 tbsp plain yogurt

1 tbsp vegetable oil, plus extra for brushing

1 tsp black onion seeds

1 tbsp chopped fresh cilantro

Sift the flour, salt, and coriander together into a bowl and stir in the garlic and yeast. Make a well in the center and pour in the honey, lukewarm water, yogurt, and oil. Stir well with a wooden spoon until the dough begins to come together, then knead with your hands until it leaves the side of the bowl. Turn out onto a lightly floured counter and knead well for about 10 minutes, until smooth and elastic.

Brush a bowl with oil. Shape the dough into a ball, put it into the bowl, and cover with a damp dish towel. Let rise in a warm place for 1–2 hours, until the dough has doubled in volume.

Put three cookie sheets into the oven and preheat to 475°F/240°C. Preheat the broiler.

Turn out the dough onto a lightly floured counter and punch down with your fist. Divide the dough into three pieces, shape each piece into a ball, and cover two of them with oiled plastic wrap. Roll out the uncovered piece of dough into a teardrop shape about ⅜ inch/8 mm thick and cover with oiled plastic wrap. Roll out the other pieces of dough in the same way.

Place the naans on the preheated cookie sheets and sprinkle with the onion seeds and chopped cilantro. Bake in the preheated oven for 5 minutes, until puffed up. Transfer the naans to the broiler pan, brush with oil, and broil for 2–3 minutes. Serve warm.

TURKISH FLATBREAD

Sift together the flour, salt, cumin, and coriander into a bowl and stir in the sugar and yeast. Make a well in the center and pour in the oil and lukewarm water. Stir well with a wooden spoon until the dough begins to come together, then knead with your hands until it leaves the side of the bowl. Turn out onto a lightly floured counter and knead well for about 10 minutes, until smooth and elastic.

Brush a bowl with oil. Shape the dough into a ball, put it into the bowl, and cover with a damp dish towel. Let rise in a warm place for 1 hour, until the dough has doubled in volume.

Lightly brush a cookie sheet with oil. Turn out the dough onto a lightly floured counter, punch down with your fist, and knead for 1–2 minutes. Divide the dough into eight equal pieces, shape each piece into a ball, then roll out to an 8-inch/20-cm round. Cover the rounds with a damp dish towel and let rest for 20 minutes.

Heat a heavy skillet and brush the bottom with oil. Add one of the dough rounds, cover, and cook for 2–3 minutes, until lightly browned on the underside. Turn over with a metal spatula, re-cover the skillet, and cook for an additional 2 minutes, until lightly browned on the second side. Remove from the skillet and cook the remaining dough rounds in the same way.

MAKES 8

6½ cups all-purpose flour, plus extra for dusting

1½ tsp salt

1 tsp ground cumin

½ tsp ground coriander

1 tsp superfine sugar

¼ oz/7 g active dry yeast

2 tbsp olive oil, plus extra for brushing

1¾ cups lukewarm water

TOMATO & ROSEMARY FOCACCIA

Sift the flour and salt together into a bowl and stir in the yeast and rosemary. Make a well in the center, pour in 4 tablespoons of the oil, and mix quickly with a wooden spoon. Gradually stir in the lukewarm water but do not overmix. Turn out onto a lightly floured counter and knead for 2 minutes. The dough will be quite wet; do not add more flour.

Brush a bowl with oil. Shape the dough into a ball, put it into the bowl, and cover with a damp dish towel. Let rise in a warm place for 2 hours, until doubled in volume.

Brush a cookie sheet with oil. Turn out the dough onto a lightly floured counter and punch down with your fist, then knead for 1 minute. Put the dough onto the prepared cookie sheet and press out into an even layer. Cover the cookie sheet with a damp dish towel and let rise in a warm place for 1 hour.

Preheat the oven to 475°F/240°C. Cut the sun-dried tomatoes into pieces. Whisk the remaining oil with a little water in a bowl. Dip your fingers into the oil mixture and press them into the dough to make dimples all over the loaf. Sprinkle with the sea salt. Press the tomato pieces into some of the dimples, drizzle with the remaining oil mixture, and sprinkle the loaf with the rosemary sprigs.

Reduce the oven temperature to 425°F/220°C and bake the focaccia for 20 minutes, until golden brown. Transfer to a wire rack to cool slightly, then serve while still warm.

MAKES 1 LOAF

- 4½ cups white bread flour, plus extra for dusting
- 1½ tsp salt
- 1½ tsp active dry yeast
- 2 tbsp chopped fresh rosemary, plus extra sprigs to garnish
- 6 tbsp extra virgin olive oil, plus extra for brushing
- 1¼ cups lukewarm water
- 6 sun-dried tomatoes in oil, drained
- 1 tsp coarse sea salt

BASIC PIZZA DOUGH

SERVES 2–4

1½ cups all-purpose flour, plus extra for dusting

1 tsp salt

1 tsp active dry yeast

1 tbsp olive oil, plus extra for brushing and drizzling

6 tbsp lukewarm water

fresh basil sprigs, to garnish

topping

¾ cup prepared pizza tomato sauce or 12 oz/350 g tomatoes, peeled and halved

1 garlic clove, thinly sliced

2 oz/55 g mozzarella cheese, thinly sliced

1 tsp dried oregano

salt and pepper

Sift the flour and salt together into a bowl and stir in the yeast. Make a well in the center and pour in the oil and lukewarm water. Stir well with a wooden spoon until the dough begins to come together, then knead with your hands until it leaves the side of the bowl. Turn out onto a lightly floured counter and knead well for 5–10 minutes, until smooth and elastic.

Brush a bowl with oil. Shape the dough into a ball, put it into the bowl, and cover with a damp dish towel. Let rise in a warm place for 1 hour, until the dough has doubled in volume.

Brush a cookie sheet with oil. Turn out the dough onto a lightly floured counter, punch down with your fist, and knead for 1 minute. Roll or press out the dough to a 10-inch/25-cm round. Place on the prepared cookie sheet and push up the edge slightly all around. Cover the cookie sheet with a damp dish towel and let rise in a warm place for 10 minutes.

Preheat the oven to 400°F/200°C. Spread the tomato sauce, if using, over the pizza bottom almost to the edge. If using fresh tomatoes, squeeze out some of the juice and coarsely chop the flesh. Spread them evenly over the pizza bottom and drizzle with oil. Sprinkle the garlic over the tomato, add the mozzarella cheese, sprinkle with the oregano, and season to taste with salt and pepper. Bake in the preheated oven for 15–20 minutes, until the crust is golden brown and crisp. Brush the crust with oil, garnish with basil sprigs, and serve immediately.

ENGLISH MUFFINS

Sift the flour and salt together into a bowl and stir in the sugar and yeast. Make a well in the center and add the lukewarm water and yogurt. Stir with a wooden spoon until the dough begins to come together, then knead with your hands until it comes away from the side of the bowl. Turn out onto a lightly floured counter and knead for 5–10 minutes, until smooth and elastic.

Brush a bowl with oil. Shape the dough into a ball, put it into the bowl, and cover with a damp dish towel. Let rise in a warm place for 30–40 minutes, until the dough has doubled in volume.

Dust a cookie sheet with flour. Turn out the dough onto a lightly floured counter and knead lightly. Roll out to a thickness of ¾ inch/2 cm. Stamp out 10–12 rounds with a 3-inch/7.5-cm cookie cutter and sprinkle each round with semolina. Transfer the muffins to the prepared cookie sheet, cover with a damp dish towel, and let rise in a warm place for 30–40 minutes.

Heat a grill pan or large skillet over medium–high heat and brush lightly with oil. Add half the muffins and cook for 7–8 minutes on each side, until golden brown. Cook the remaining muffins in the same way.

MAKES 10–12

4 cups white bread flour, plus extra for dusting

½ tsp salt

1 tsp superfine sugar

1½ tsp active dry yeast

generous 1 cup lukewarm water

½ cup plain yogurt

vegetable oil, for brushing

¼ cup semolina

BAGELS

Sift the flour and salt together into a bowl and stir in the yeast. Make a well in the center, pour in the egg and lukewarm water, and mix to a dough. Turn out onto a lightly floured counter and knead well for about 10 minutes, until smooth.

Brush a bowl with oil. Shape the dough into a ball, place it in the bowl, and cover with a damp dish towel. Let rise in a warm place for 1 hour, until the dough has doubled in volume.

Brush two cookie sheets with oil and dust a baking sheet with flour. Turn out the dough onto a lightly floured counter and punch down with your fist. Knead for 2 minutes, then divide into ten pieces. Shape each piece into a ball and let rest for 5 minutes. Gently flatten each ball with a lightly floured hand and make a hole in the center with the handle of a wooden spoon. Put the bagels on the floured sheet, cover with a damp dish towel, and let rise in a warm place for 20 minutes.

Meanwhile, preheat the oven to 425°F/220°C and bring a large saucepan of water to a boil. Reduce the heat until the water is barely simmering, then add two bagels. Poach for 1 minute, then turn over, and poach for 30 seconds more. Remove with a slotted spoon and drain on a dish towel. Poach the remaining bagels in the same way.

Transfer the bagels to the oiled cookie sheets. Beat the egg white with the water in a bowl and brush it over the bagels. Sprinkle with the caraway seeds and bake in the preheated oven for 25–30 minutes, until golden brown. Transfer to a wire rack to cool.

MAKES 10

3 cups white bread flour, plus extra for dusting

2 tsp salt

¼ oz/7 g active dry yeast

1 tbsp lightly beaten egg

scant 1 cup lukewarm water

vegetable oil, for brushing

1 egg white

2 tsp water

2 tbsp caraway seeds

BREADSTICKS

MAKES 30

generous 2⅛ cups white bread flour, plus extra for dusting

1½ tsp salt

1½ tsp active dry yeast

scant 1 cup lukewarm water

3 tbsp olive oil, plus extra for oiling and brushing

sesame seeds, for coating

Lightly oil two cookie sheets. Sift the flour and salt together into a warmed bowl. Stir in the yeast. Make a well in the center. Add the water and oil to the well and mix to form a soft dough.

Turn out the dough onto a lightly floured counter and knead for 5–10 minutes, or until smooth and elastic. Put the dough in an oiled bowl, cover with a damp dish towel, and let rise in a warm place for 1 hour, or until doubled in size.

Turn out the dough again and knead lightly. Roll out to a rectangle measuring 9 x 8 inches/23 x 20 cm. Cut the dough into three strips, each 8 inches/20 cm long, then cut each strip across into ten equal pieces.

Gently roll and stretch each piece of dough into a stick about 12 inches/30 cm long, then brush with oil. Spread the sesame seeds out on a large shallow plate or tray. Roll each breadstick in the sesame seeds to coat, then place them, spaced well apart, on the prepared cookie sheets. Brush with oil, cover with a damp dish towel, and let rise in a warm place for 15 minutes. Preheat the oven to 400°F/200°C.

Bake the breadsticks in the preheated oven for 10 minutes. Turn over and bake for an additional 5–10 minutes, until golden. Transfer to a wire rack and let cool.

CHEESE STRAWS

Sift the flour, salt, and curry powder into a bowl. Add the butter and rub in until the mixture resembles breadcrumbs. Add the cheese and half the egg and mix to form a dough. Wrap in plastic wrap and chill in the refrigerator for 30 minutes.

Preheat the oven to 400°F/200°C, then grease several cookie sheets. On a floured counter, roll out the dough to ¼ inch/5 mm thick. Cut into 3 x ½-inch/7.5 x 1-cm strips. Pinch the strips lightly along the sides and place on the prepared cookie sheets.

Brush the strips with the remaining egg and sprinkle half with poppy seeds and half with cumin seeds. Bake in the preheated oven for 10–15 minutes, or until golden. Transfer to wire racks to cool.

MAKES 24

generous ¾ cup all-purpose flour, plus extra for dusting

pinch of salt

1 tsp curry powder

4 tbsp butter, plus extra for greasing

½ cup grated cheddar cheese

1 egg, beaten

poppy and cumin seeds, for sprinkling

SAVORY OAT CRACKERS

Preheat the oven to 350°F/180°C and lightly grease two cookie sheets.

Rub the butter into the oats and flour using your fingertips. Stir in the salt, thyme, and walnuts, then add the egg and mix to a soft dough. Break off walnut-size pieces of dough and roll into balls, then roll in sesame seeds to coat lightly and evenly.

Place the balls of dough on the prepared cookie sheets, spacing them well apart, and roll the rolling pin over them to flatten as much as possible. Bake in the preheated oven for 12–15 minutes, or until firm and pale golden in color.

Cool on the cookie sheets for 3–4 minutes, then transfer to a wire rack to finish cooling.

MAKES 12–14

scant ½ cup unsalted butter, plus extra for greasing

scant 1 cup rolled oats

¼ cup whole wheat flour

½ tsp coarse salt

1 tsp dried thyme

⅓ cup walnuts, finely chopped

1 egg, beaten

3 tbsp sesame seeds

CHEESE SABLÉS

MAKES 35

generous 1 cup all-purpose flour,
  plus extra for dusting

1½ cups grated sharp cheddar
  cheese

⅔ cup butter, cut into small
  pieces, plus extra for greasing

1 egg yolk

sesame seeds, for sprinkling

Mix the flour and grated cheese together in a bowl. Add the butter to the cheese and flour mixture and rub in with your fingertips until combined.

Stir in the egg yolk and mix to form a dough. Wrap the dough and chill in the refrigerator for about 30 minutes.

Preheat the oven to 400°F/200°C. Lightly grease several cookie sheets.

On a lightly floured counter, roll out the dough thinly. Stamp out rounds using a 2½-inch/6-cm cookie cutter, re-rolling the trimmings to make about 35 rounds in total.

Carefully transfer the dough rounds onto the prepared cookie sheets and sprinkle the sesame seeds evenly over the top of them.

Bake in the preheated oven for 10 minutes, until the sablés are lightly golden. Transfer the cheese sablés to a wire rack with a spatula and let cool slightly before serving.

CHEESE & MUSTARD SCONES

Preheat the oven to 425°F/220°C. Lightly grease a cookie sheet.

Sift the flour, baking powder, and salt into a mixing bowl. Rub in the butter with your fingertips until the mixture resembles breadcrumbs.

Stir in the cheese, mustard, and enough milk to form a soft dough.

On a lightly floured counter, knead the dough very lightly, then flatten it out with the palm of your hand to a depth of about 1 inch/2.5 cm.

Cut the dough into eight wedges with a knife. Brush each one with a little milk and sprinkle with pepper to taste.

Bake in the preheated oven for 10–15 minutes, until golden brown. Transfer the scones to a wire rack and let cool slightly before serving.

MAKES 8

4 tbsp butter, cut into small pieces, plus extra for greasing

generous 1½ cups self-rising flour, plus extra for dusting

1 tsp baking powder

pinch of salt

1½ cups grated sharp cheddar cheese

1 tsp mustard powder

⅔ cup milk, plus extra for brushing

pepper

PARMESAN & PINE NUT MUFFINS

Preheat the oven to 400°F/200°C. Grease a 12-cup muffin pan or line with 12 muffin paper liners.

To make the topping, mix together the Parmesan cheese and pine nuts and set aside.

To make the muffins, sift together the flour, baking powder, salt, and pepper to taste into a large bowl. Stir in the Parmesan cheese and pine nuts.

Lightly beat the eggs in a large pitcher or bowl, then beat in the buttermilk and oil. Make a well in the center of the dry ingredients and pour in the beaten liquid ingredients. Stir gently until just combined; do not overmix.

Spoon the batter into the prepared muffin pan. Scatter the topping over the muffins. Bake in the preheated oven for about 20 minutes, until well risen, golden brown, and firm to the touch.

Let the muffins cool in the pan for 5 minutes, then serve warm.

MAKES 12

oil or melted butter, for greasing (if using)

2 cups all-purpose flour

1 tbsp baking powder

⅛ tsp salt

¾ cup freshly grated Parmesan cheese

½ cup pine nuts

2 large eggs

1 cup buttermilk

6 tbsp sunflower oil or melted, cooled butter

pepper

topping

4 tsp freshly grated Parmesan cheese

¼ cup pine nuts

CARAMELIZED ONION MUFFINS

MAKES 12

oil or melted butter, for greasing (optional)

7 tbsp sunflower oil

3 onions, finely chopped

1 tbsp red wine vinegar

2 tsp sugar

2 cups all-purpose flour

1 tbsp baking powder

⅛ tsp salt

2 large eggs

1 cup buttermilk

pepper

Preheat the oven to 400°F/200°C. Grease a 12-cup muffin pan or line with 12 muffin paper liners.

Heat 2 tablespoons of the oil in a skillet. Add the onions and cook for about 3 minutes, until beginning to soften. Add the vinegar and sugar and cook, stirring occasionally, for an additional 10 minutes, until golden brown. Remove from the heat and let cool.

Meanwhile, sift together the flour, baking powder, salt, and pepper to taste into a large bowl.

Lightly beat the eggs in a large pitcher or bowl, then beat in the buttermilk and the remaining oil. Make a well in the center of the dry ingredients, pour in the beaten liquid ingredients, and add the onion mixture, reserving 4 tablespoons for the topping. Stir gently until just combined; do not overmix.

Spoon the batter into the prepared muffin pan. Sprinkle the reserved onion mixture over the tops of the muffins. Bake in the preheated oven for about 20 minutes, until well risen, golden brown, and firm to the touch.

Let the muffins cool in the pan for 5 minutes, then serve warm.

TRIPLE TOMATO TART

To make the puff pastry, sift the flour and salt into a large bowl and rub in 2 tablespoons of the butter. Gradually add the water, just enough to bring the pastry together, and knead to form a smooth dough. Wrap the dough and let chill for 30 minutes.

Wrap the remaining butter in plastic wrap and shape it into a 1¼ inch/3 cm thick rectangle. Roll out the dough to a rectangle three times longer and 1¼ inches/3 cm wider than the butter and place the butter in the center with the long side toward you. Fold over the "wings" of dough to enclose the butter—press down the edges to seal and then turn the dough so the short side faces you. Roll the dough to its original length, fold into three, turn, and roll again to its original length. Repeat this once more, then rewrap the dough and let chill again for 30 minutes. Remove from the refrigerator and repeat the rolling and turning twice more. Let chill again for 30 minutes.

Preheat the oven to 375°F/190°C. Roll out the dough to 14 x 10 inches/35 x 25 cm and lift onto a baking sheet. Spread the tomato paste over the dough, leaving a 1¼-inch/3-cm margin around the edge. Arrange the tomato slices over the tomato paste, sprinkle over the tomato halves, top with the rosemary, and drizzle with 1 tablespoon of the oil and the vinegar. Brush the edges of the dough with the egg yolk and bake in the preheated oven for 10 minutes. Sprinkle over the salami and bake for an additional 10–15 minutes. Remove from the oven and season to taste with salt and pepper. Drizzle with the remaining oil and garnish with thyme.

SERVES 6

puff pastry
1⅛ cups all-purpose flour

pinch of salt

¾ cup unsalted butter

about ⅔ cup chilled water

(or use 9 oz/250 g prepared puff pastry)

topping
3 tbsp sun-dried tomato paste

9 oz/250 g ripe vine tomatoes, sliced

5½ oz/150 g cherry tomatoes, cut in half

2 fresh rosemary sprigs, chopped

2 tbsp extra virgin olive oil

1 tbsp balsamic vinegar

1 egg yolk

4½ oz/125 g Italian sliced salami, chopped

salt and pepper

fresh thyme sprigs, to garnish

FETA & SPINACH TARTLETS

Grease six 3½-inch/9-cm loose-bottom fluted tart pans. Sift the flour and salt into a food processor, add the butter, and process until the mixture resembles fine breadcrumbs. Tip the mixture into a large bowl and add the nutmeg and enough of the cold water to bring the dough together.

Turn out onto a floured counter and divide into six equal-size pieces. Roll each piece to fit the tart pans. Carefully place each piece of dough in its pan and press well to fit the pan. Roll the rolling pin over the pan to neaten the edges and trim the excess dough. Cut six pieces of parchment paper and fit a piece into each tart, fill with dried beans, and let chill in the refrigerator for 30 minutes. Meanwhile, preheat the oven to 400°F/200°C.

Bake the tart shells blind in the preheated oven for 10 minutes, then remove the beans and paper.

Blanch the spinach in boiling water for just 1 minute, then drain and press to squeeze out all the water. Chop the spinach. Melt the butter in a skillet, add the spinach, and cook gently to evaporate any remaining liquid. Season well with salt and pepper. Stir in the cream and egg yolks. Divide the feta cheese among the tarts, top with the spinach mixture, and bake for 10 minutes. Sprinkle the pine nuts over the tartlets and cook for an additional 5 minutes.

MAKES 6

pie dough
generous ¾ cup all-purpose flour, plus extra for dusting

pinch of salt

5 tbsp cold butter, cut into pieces, plus extra for greasing

½ tsp ground nutmeg

1–2 tbsp cold water

filling
6 cups baby spinach

2 tbsp butter

⅔ cup heavy cream

3 egg yolks

generous 1 cup crumbled feta cheese

scant ⅓ cup pine nuts

salt and pepper

QUICHE LORRAINE

SERVES 6

pie dough

1¾ cups all-purpose flour, plus extra for dusting

scant ½ cup butter

1–2 tbsp cold water

filling

1 tbsp butter

1 small onion, finely chopped

4 lean bacon strips, diced

½ cup grated Gruyère cheese or cheddar cheese

2 eggs, beaten

1¼ cups light cream

pepper

For the pie dough, sift the flour into a bowl and rub in the butter with your fingertips until the mixture resembles fine breadcrumbs. Stir in just enough water to bind the mixture to a firm dough.

Roll out the dough on a lightly floured counter to a round slightly larger than a 9-inch/23-cm loose-bottom round tart pan, 1¼ inches/3 cm deep. Lift the dough onto the pan and press it down into the fluted edge, using the back of your finger. Roll the rolling pin over the edge of the pan to trim off the excess dough. Prick the bottom all over with a fork. Chill in the refrigerator for at least 10 minutes to let the dough rest and prevent shrinkage.

Preheat the oven to 400°C/200°C and preheat a baking sheet. Place a sheet of parchment paper in the pie shell. Fill with dried beans to weigh it down. Place on the baking sheet and bake in the preheated oven for 10 minutes. Remove the paper and beans and bake for an additional 10 minutes.

For the filling, melt the butter in a skillet and cook the onion and bacon over medium heat for about 5 minutes, stirring occasionally, until the onion is softened and lightly browned. Spread the mixture evenly in the hot pie shell and sprinkle with half the cheese. Beat together the eggs and cream in a small bowl and season to taste with pepper. Pour into the pie shell and sprinkle with the remaining cheese.

Reduce the oven temperature to 375°F/190°C. Place the quiche in the oven and bake for 25–30 minutes, or until golden brown and just set. Let cool for 10 minutes before turning out. Serve warm or cold.

INDEX